The
Things to Say
to Get the
Job You Want

THE JOB
Interview
PHRASE BOOK

NANCY SCHUMAN,
CSP, VICE PRESIDENT LLOYD STAFFING

Aadamsmedia
Avon, Massachusetts

Published by
Adams Media, a division of F+W Media, Inc.
57 Littlefield Street, Avon, MA 02322. U.S.A.
www.adamsmedia.com

ISBN 10: 1-4405-0184-X
ISBN 13: 978-1-4405-0184-5

Printed in the United States of America.

J I H G F E D C

Library of Congress Cataloging-in-Publication Data
is available from the publisher.

This publication is designed to provide accurate and authoritative
information with regard to the subject matter covered. It is sold with
the understanding that the publisher is not engaged in rendering legal,
accounting, or other professional advice. If legal advice or other expert
assistance is required, the services of a competent professional person
should be sought.
—From a *Declaration of Principles* jointly adopted by a Committee
of the American Bar Association and a Committee of
Publishers and Associations

Many of the designations used by manufacturers and sellers to distinguish their product are claimed as trademarks. Where those designations appear in this book and Adams Media was aware of a trademark
claim, the designations have been printed with initial capital letters.

This book is available at quantity discounts for bulk purchases.
For information, please call 1-800-289-0963.

Contents

Introduction

If you've picked up this book, you've most likely landed an interview. Congratulations! Now comes the work of preparing for whatever questions you might be asked. Every interview is different—mostly because every interviewer has a different idea of the types of questions they'll ask you. Some may focus on your past work experience without getting into personal details, and others may rely on personal questions to help them figure out if you're a good fit for the company. You need to be ready for any type of question that comes your way. That's where *The Job Interview Phrase Book* comes in handy.

Divided into ten chapters, *The Job Interview Phrase Book* is a concise guide suitable for new and seasoned job seekers alike. Chapter 1 reviews basic etiquette and how to get an interview off to a good start. The following chapters walk you through pairs of questions and answers on topics ranging from your skills, accomplishments, and career goals to your business sense, interest in the company, and education. You'll learn how to handle tough questions about your career. Not sure what to say when asked about a bad boss? Wondering how to explain to a potential employer that you were fired? Whether you've been unemployed for months or years, held numerous jobs in a short period of time, or are applying for a job outside of your industry, this book will steer you in the right direction with clear answers that you can deliver with confidence. Each question and answer is followed by a brief synopsis that explains why the given answer is appropriate and how it will help you stand out to your interviewer. To help prevent you from getting tongue-tied when asked about your age, religion, or political views, a section on illegal questions helps you respond appropriately without giving away information that is no one's business but your own. A final chapter lists popular buzz words and phrases according to industry. You can use the language in this section during interviews or even apply it to your resume.

A job interview is a chance to talk about what you've accomplished in your career and why you're ready to move on to a new opportunity. No one knows you better than yourself, so make sure you're able to present yourself in the best light possible. Use *The Job Interview Phrase Book* to prepare and practice—and ultimately get the job!

Chapter 1

Preparing for the **Interview**

HAVE YOU EVER WONDERED WHAT THE POINT OF A JOB INTERVIEW IS? THE employer has your resume. Can't she just look at it to see whether you have the necessary skills and experience? All she should need to do is make a phone call or two to verify that information, right? While it is made up of information about your past experience, your resume doesn't give the employer a full picture of who you are. Your resume is only a summary of your skills, work experience, and educational background. With only your resume to rely on, the person interviewing you won't have any idea of the specific things about you that will set you apart from the other candidates.

After all, a resume is merely a piece of paper, and you are so much more than that. An interviewer can't learn about someone's personality by looking at a resume. She can't discover how a candidate developed some of his skills or which accomplishments meant the most to him. The interviewer can't find out how the candidate reacts to change or adversity by reading his resume.

The only way an interviewer can learn any of those things about a job candidate is by talking to him and asking questions. This will allow the candidate to paint a picture of himself that is much more elaborate than what can fit on one sheet of paper.

Preparing to Answer Questions

You will be asked a variety of questions on a job interview. These questions will pertain to your skills and abilities, accomplishments, education, and work history. You will also be asked questions about your strengths and weaknesses, your interests and hobbies, and your likes and dislikes, all of which will allow the employer to learn about your personal traits or characteristics.

In the chapters that follow, you will find answers and key phrases to use when responding to questions you might encounter on a job interview. Use them as a guideline. While you should not go into a job interview with a memorized script, you should have an idea of how you will answer most questions that will come your way. Chapter 9 gives you ideas for the types of questions you should ask the interviewer. Use these questions in the same way— as a guideline to be adapted to your particular situation and the company and industry you are interviewing with.

▶ Be Specific

On a job interview, you will be asked questions about your skills, for example. Of course, you know what skills you have, but can you discuss how you acquired them? What if you're asked about your accomplishments? You've no doubt accomplished a lot at work, but can you recall specifics? You need anecdotes that clearly back up your claims, so it is imperative that you prepare in advance and have some good examples of your strengths ready when the subject comes up.

▶ Take Time to Rehearse

In preparing for job interviews it is important that you do some practice interviewing, both alone and with others. Rehearsing for interviews will allow you to work on any problems that may be viewed as negatives by the interviewer. Rehearsing will also allow you to become more comfortable with the interview process. By the time you go on an interview, you will have no problem confidently answering questions.

The First Defining Moments

The first minute or two of any interview is the most crucial. As the saying goes, you only get one chance to make a great first impression, and this is when you want to do just that. Your goal is to wow the interviewer and make a favorable impression that will give you an edge over some of your rivals and open the door to an offer of employment.

▶ Introducing Yourself

When the interviewer arrives, it's show time. If you appear shy or intimidated, an interviewer may not want to dig too deep and embarrass you; that said, she will not ask you the really difficult questions—the questions that get you the job. It's human nature to judge a person by their first impression; it's that first impression that hooks many of us when we fall in love. You and your interviewer do not need to fall in love, but you do need to fall "in like." It shouldn't be difficult to do this, as long as you know what the interviewer is looking for.

▶ Maintaining Eye Contact

When the time for your interview arrives and you get the chance to meet the person who will be grilling you for the next hour or so, stand up and greet him with a warm smile and maintain constant eye contact during your articulate introduction. Establishing eye contact is probably one of the most important parts of your introduction. You want to make sure that you look the interviewer directly in the eye as you are being introduced and/or shake hands. At the same time, you don't want to make him uncomfortable, so be sure not to stare.

▶ **Have a Firm Handshake**

Similar limitations are placed on the handshake; while you don't want your handshake to be so light that the interviewer is forced to check for a pulse, you also don't want to be so enthusiastic that she winds up in the emergency room with a fracture. In your pre-interview sessions with a friend, practice your handshake so that you will be able to offer up a firm grip with a quick shake or two of the hand. Then, don't hold on for dear life; let go.

Starting Off on the Right Foot

Before getting down to the important stuff—like why you would do well with this company—it is likely that the interviewer will engage you in a bit of small talk to get the conversation flowing. Prepare for these questions as well. Don't mistake, for example, "How was your ride in?" or "Did you have any problem finding us?" for anything other than small talk. The interviewer really is not interested in whether or not you hit any traffic or encountered any accidents on your way to the office. If you anticipate simple questions like these, you can be better prepared to answer them without bogging down the flow of conversation.

All too often, job seekers make the mistake of launching into a huge dialogue about how long it took them to get to the office, how they found a great short cut, and so on. The last thing an interviewer wants—or needs—in response to these initial questions is anything longer than "Great," "Fine," or "No problem!" Don't be verbose; it can cause the interviewer to question your suitability to the company immediately. Also, regardless of how nervous you may be, don't let small-talk questions like these dumbfound you. After all, if you have trouble answering a simple question about the weather, how are you going to help this company come up with a winning marketing strategy?

Upon arriving at the interviewer's office or area of your destination, wait until the interviewer tells you to be seated before sitting, then sit (don't plunk) on the designated chair or sofa. Stick with that chair or sofa even if it proves to be uncomfortable. In fact, you don't want to be too comfortable. You want to keep alert, not doze off!

Be on your best behavior. The traditional rules of etiquette should be observed at all times during a job interview. Don't yawn, chew gum, or fidget. A few more things could be added to this list:

- Don't mimic the body language or mannerisms of the interviewer. (This can happen when you get nervous.)
- Don't keep looking at your watch.
- Don't be negative.
- Don't talk too much.
- Don't ask about money, perks, or things that are unrelated to the job or company at hand.
- Don't move or touch anything on the interviewer's desk. This office is his "home," and you wouldn't want a stranger to touch things in your home.

If your interview is going well and you are sure this is a job you want, don't be afraid to say so. Sometimes candidates who seem to be perfect for the job are passed over simply because they never let the interviewer know they wanted it.

Don't let this happen to you. Don't be afraid to be proactive, and don't be bashful. Wrap up your interview by giving some of the reasons you like the company before asking about your prospects. Make it clear that you think this job was made for you and vice versa.

Set a Tone

The tone of the meeting depends on the personality of the interviewer. He may ask a straight line of professional questions, or he may be more lighthearted and laid back. Regardless of the manner of the interviewer, you should always prepare your answers in a very professional way.

One mistake that candidates often make is to prepare for each question by brainstorming the "perfect" answer. They think about the kind of answer the perfect candidate would give and use that. In most of these instances, the job seeker is wasting the company's time. Trying to project the perfect image can only result in disaster because often the interviewer sees right through it. On the other hand, if the interviewer buys into the candidate's perfect persona, she may be surprised when—once hired—the candidate does not perform as perfectly as expected.

Though you shouldn't highlight your faults to the employer, neither should you pretend to be someone or something you are not. Many career experts think that the best way to set and maintain a professional tone throughout an interview is to create a sort of job interview persona. Think about the many personal traits a job interviewer would be interested in and be sure to project those characteristics. Which of your traits would make you a strong candidate and set you apart from the rest of the candidates? Think about the many successful people you know or have heard about and the personality traits that make them good leaders. How can you convey to the interviewer that these qualifications are part of your own professional nature?

Think of yourself as a calm, cool, and collected individual; be relaxed enough to allow a bit of your personality into the conversation. With any luck, your research has provided you with an understanding of the company's vision. If you can link this vision to your own personal vision for your career, you should make a strong impression on your interviewer.

Remember, however, that in the end you have no control over the outcome of an interview; you do not decide whether or not you get the job. In many cases, you could conduct yourself perfectly throughout the interview and still not get the job. On the other hand, you could feel like you've botched the entire interview and still receive an offer.

The only thing you do have control over during the interview is what you do and say while you're there. Always keep the following key qualities an interviewer is looking for in the back of your mind and be sure to convey your aptitude in each of them:

- Adaptability
- Competence
- Confidence
- Creativity
- Dedication
- Dependability
- Easygoing nature
- Enthusiasm
- Leadership ability
- Motivation
- Problem-solving ability
- Resourcefulness

Think of these qualities in every answer you give and everything you say, and you should have no problem projecting the image of a confident and competent candidate.

Chapter 2

Discussing Your **Skills** and **Experience**

Now that you understand how to present a professional image and confidently interact with your interviewer, it's time to think about what you'll say when your interviewer starts asking questions.

This chapter focuses on responses you should give when questioned about your specific skills, work experience, and personal interests. Skills can be divided into two categories: hard skills and soft skills. Hard skills, or technical skills, are the ones that define your job. You will be required to be proficient in these skills, and your prospective employer will want you to prove this to him by drawing on specific examples of how you have used your skills. Soft skills, also known as functional or personal skills, are those skills that you need to have in order to excel at work in general. These are very wide-ranging skills. They aren't specific to any occupation, but instead they are the things that enhance your performance regardless of what your actual job is. Examples of soft skills include decision-making, time management, delegating, multitasking, and problem solving.

You may be asked questions about your work style or strengths and weaknesses. The answers you give will help the interviewer decide whether to hire you. By revealing aspects of your personality, you give a strong indication of whether you will make a good employee. The interviewer wants to know what makes you a better choice than another candidate with the same experience and skills.

Key Skills and Abilities

 What are your key skills?

*How to **answer** it: After spending the past six years as a senior systems analyst, I've developed a number of important skills, including business modeling, process re-engineering, software-package evaluation, and advanced programming capabilities in UNIX and C environments. I was very pleased to discover that these are the skills you are seeking. Would you like to hear about specific examples of my work?*

Talk about your key skills and how you'll use them in this job. Avoid using clichés or generalities. Offer specific evidence, drawing parallels between your current or previous job and the job you're interviewing for. Don't be afraid to ask a question in your answer. However, the last thing you want to do is seem garrulous, so find out if the interviewer would like to hear specific examples and, if so, oblige her.

 What skills do you think are most critical to this job?

*How to **answer** it: As technology is ever changing, I think that it is important to keep up with the latest marketing trends. Knowing what kinds of new technologies exist and how to go about incorporating them into my own marketing plans is what will keep me ahead of the competition. Creativity is also of major importance to the marketing industry; new ideas can quickly become stale and stagnant. A successful marketing associate will always be looking ahead to the next big*

revolution. If, just a few years ago, I had not been aware of the important role that the web would play in our day-to-day duties, my current company could have been wiped out by the competition.

When describing the skills you feel are most important, make sure that you know how these skills relate to the position at hand. Illustrate how the cited skills have helped you in your current and/or past positions.

Q: **If you were to stay in your current job, what kinds of tasks would you spend more time on and why?**

*How to **answer** it: If I were to stay at my current job, I'd like to gain more experience in labor negotiating. In particular, I'd like to help negotiate labor contracts, resolve grievances at the step-4 level, and prepare grievances for arbitration. Though I have a very strong background in all areas of human resources, I believe that a strong grasp of labor relations experience will round out my skills so that I could have the opportunity to move up to a position of department head and possibly vice president.*

In answering this question, think about the aspects of your job that interest you most. What are the areas you would like to strengthen and advance in? What are the areas you need work in so that you could advance? Talk about the current responsibilities that give you the most satisfaction. Another smart move (and one that will score you points in the motivation department) is to talk about the possibility of advancement. Again, make sure your goals are realistic. Talk about the career path you are heading down and how the sharpening of certain skills can help you attain your goals.

Q: **What skills would you like to develop in this job?**

How to **answer** *it: I'd like to develop my negotiating skills. I've had considerable experience interpreting and implementing large contracts, but I've been limited in negotiating the actual conditions, costs, and standards for a major contract. I believe this job will offer me the opportunity to be a member of a negotiating team so I can begin acquiring the skills necessary to lead the team.*

Make sure you are not inhabiting an imaginary world in your answer to this question! First, your answer should coincide with skills that this job will help you develop. Second, you should have already covered some of the prerequisites to developing the skills you mention. For example, you wouldn't want to apply for a job as a receptionist with the Joffrey Ballet and say that you hope to develop your ballet skills.

Answering this question gives you an opportunity to talk a little bit about all your different skills. Discuss your hard (technical) skills, such as your computer knowledge and customer service skills. It's also important to focus on the soft skills you'd like to develop. Describe your functional skills, such as organizing, problem solving, writing, listening, and communicating, as well as personal skills, such as how well you work with others, whether or not you are able to assert authority, and how well you manage your time.

Q: **How well do you write?**

How to **answer** *it: I would say that my writing skills are above average. I made a very conscious effort to develop these skills while I was working toward my MBA. I even took an entrepreneurial class in which the chief assignment was to develop, write, and continually rewrite a business plan. I have brought it along if you would like to see it.*

A great way to prepare for an interview is to overprepare. If you anticipate a question such as this one, bring along a sample of your work. For more creative positions (photographer, copywriter, graphic artist, and so on), always be sure to pack your portfolio so that the interviewer can see your work and assess your talent for himself. Even if the job you are applying for is not creative in nature, there may be some writing involved. A sharp set of writing skills is always a great asset.

Q: Could you tell me a little bit about your computer skills?

*How to **answer** it: I would consider myself very well versed when it comes to computers. In my current position, I typically use Microsoft Word, PowerPoint, and Excel. I am also familiar with various graphic design programs, including Quark, Photoshop, and Adobe Illustrator. I have some experience with Macintosh systems as well. I am a pro when it comes to navigating the Internet and have even picked up a bit of knowledge as far as HTML programming goes.*

Computer literacy is a must in today's job market, no matter what the position. A working knowledge of a word processing program such as Microsoft Word is essential, and familiarity with database management or graphics programs is valuable as well. If your computer experience is rather limited, have a friend tutor you in an MS Office Suite application, or visit the local library and try to find your way around some of the most basic word processing programs. These programs are simple to learn and will allow you to avoid having to say that you have very limited or no computer skills. You must be web savvy and have a knowledge of e-mail. Windows remains the dominant platform in the workforce, but Macintosh environments are prevalent in creative fields such as advertising, publishing, and design.

Q: How are your presentation skills? How do you prepare for presentations?

*How to **answer** it: I didn't always like making presentations, but since I had to make a lot of them on my last two jobs, I've gotten very good at it. I do a lot of research before any presentation. I try to find out as much as possible about the client, the market they are trying to reach, their competitors, and the industry. Sometimes, if the budget allows for it, I hire an expert to help me with the research.*

This candidate answered honestly. He knows it's not that unusual to dislike presentations, so he's not afraid to admit that. It also gives him the opportunity to show off his experience and how it has gotten him over his fear. In addition, he knows the importance of having good information and knows what resources he needs to use to get it.

Q: How do your skills relate to this job?

*How to **answer** it: I am very organized, I work well on a team, and I have very good communication skills. Although I haven't worked in this field before, I know these skills will make me a valuable employee.*

Although this applicant is new to the field, she has some very desirable skills, which she makes a point of letting the interviewer know.

Q: Tell me about a crisis you encountered at work and how you handled it.

*How to **answer** it: Last year a virus was causing our computers to send out thousands of e-mail messages to our clients. We were being inundated with angry phone calls before we even knew what was going on. Our technical support person* *was on vacation, so I made a few phone calls and found some-one to fix the problem. Then I drafted an apology that was sent out by e-mail to our clients.*

This answer is good because the candidate clearly describes the problem and gives specifics on how she solved it. In addition, the crisis is one that could have caused her boss to lose clients, something that would strike fear into the hearts of most employers, including the one interviewing her.

Q: How do you manage your time?

*How to **answer** it: I prioritize my work. I figure out what needs to get done first, next, and so on. Then I calculate how much time I will need to spend on each activity or project. I set a schedule for myself and get going.*

This applicant has a plan. He knows how to prioritize and apportion the proper amount of time to each activity.

Q: Have you ever had to juggle two or more projects at the same time?

*How to **answer** it: That happened all the time on my last job. Several months ago, I was in the midst of working on one huge project for one of my bosses, when my other boss came to me with another project that needed to be completed in two days. After evaluating the second project, I realized I could complete it in a day. Since I still had about a week before the deadline for the first project, I decided to get started on the second one. I completed it by the end of the next day and went back to my first project.*

The interviewer asked for an example and this candidate gave one. He demonstrates how his ability to prioritize helped him.

How do you manage stress in your daily work?

*How to **answer** it: Unless I have a ton of work to do that I just can't get away from, I make sure that when I take my lunch hour, I actually leave the office. Just that simple change of scenery, even for a few minutes, is enough to keep me energized for the rest of the day.*

This is a simple enough question to answer. The interviewer is interested in whether you have a tendency to crack under pressure. She wants to know how you manage high-pressure situations. If you have a simple daily ritual that helps you maintain your composure, even in stressful situations, tell her about it. But beware of how that stress buster might be perceived. A power nap ritual—even on your lunch hour—could mistakenly be construed as sleeping on the job. It may also be helpful to describe a stressful project you've worked on and the specific actions you took to get it done without losing your head. If you think that your ways of relieving stress—yelling at those who hold lower positions, watching a movie in the middle of the work day—would be frowned upon by your current boss or a future one, do yourself a favor and keep it to yourself. The key is to talk about how you stay professional when under a lot of pressure.

 As assistant to the director of human resources, employees will come to you if they feel their supervisor has discriminated against them in some way. How will you handle these complaints?

*How to **answer** it: As an HR professional I know the importance of being well versed in the laws that affect the workplace. First, I will interview the employee, asking for an explanation of exactly what happened. Then, I'll interview the supervisor and get his or her side of the story.*

This candidate will take a balanced look at the situation. He will evaluate it using his knowledge of employment law and then try to solve the problem.

 You have many of the skills we're looking for. However, we also need someone with very strong sales skills. I don't see anything on your resume that indicates that you have that kind of experience.

*How to **answer** it: It's true that I don't have any formal experience in sales. I do have some informal experience, however. I ran the book fair at my son's school for the past few years. I also sold jewelry that a friend made. We rented tables at craft fairs all over the region.*

While a candidate can't make up experience, she should draw on unpaid or volunteer experience that demonstrates her skills.

 Are you good at doing research?

*How to **answer** it: I haven't done a great deal of research at work, but I do a lot of it on my own. Before I make any major purchases, take any medication, or go on vacation, I do a lot of research. I'm very good at it. The librarians at my local library are a great resource, so I make sure to go to them when I need help.*

It would have been nice if this job candidate could have drawn on work experience to highlight her research skills, but since she couldn't, she did the next best thing. She has given examples of what kind of research she has done and how she does it.

 I see from your resume this isn't your first job working in a medical office. What skills did you pick up on your two previous jobs that you think would help you on this job?

*How to **answer** it: When you described the job to me, you said you needed someone who was good with patients. You also said you wanted someone who knows a lot about the different insurance plans. My primary responsibility at both these jobs was billing. I had to deal with insurance companies every day. I found that if I learned how each one worked, it was a lot easier for the doctors in my practice to get paid and for patients to get reimbursed. I also worked at the reception desk at these jobs. Many patients who came in were clearly anxious. I was happy to be able to calm them down and hopefully offer some reassurance.*

This candidate listened to what the employer said and was able to clearly state how her skills would fill this medical practice's needs.

Interpersonal Skills

Q: What personal characteristics do you think add to your overall effectiveness?

*How to **answer** it: I think that I have a strong ability to create deeper relationships with people than business usually allows for. I am able to know more about a client than just the amount of money she brings to my company each year. I get to know my clients on a more personal level, and I keep them in mind all the time. If I read an article that I know one of my clients might enjoy, I'll send the clip along. In doing so, I find that my phone calls are returned much more quickly—and happily— than the next person's might be.*

What is it about your personal style that makes you unique from the other candidates that the interviewer has met with? What traits do you possess that make you more effective? Without sounding cocky or exploitative, talk about why you think you are able to get cooperation from others.

 What type of people do you work with most effectively?

*How to **answer** it: My favorite type of coworker is someone who is not afraid to voice her opinion. I love to work with people who are creative and willing to brainstorm ideas before deciding upon a particular solution. Confidence is always important as well.*

The key here—and in every question, really—is to remain positive. Far too many people answer this question in a way that fails to highlight the positive points they like in their coworkers; instead they drone on and on about the things they hate. A negative attitude is never in a job description, and it's certainly not something you should convey—either intentionally or unintentionally—during an interview. Make sure the company would approve of the characteristics you are describing. For example, if you are a bit of a chatterbox, you might love to have a few other talkative people in your department, but this is not the type of thing you should mention in your interview. Always remember that the interviewer is interested in how well you will fit in with the company's other employees, not how well they'll fit in with you.

Unfortunately every office has personality conflicts. What do you do when you work with someone you don't particularly like?

*How to **answer** it: While I know you don't have to be buddies with everyone you work with, workplaces are more productive if coworkers get along. I would try to resolve my differences with that person. If that wasn't possible, I'd find something about that person I could admire and respect and I'd focus on that instead of the things I didn't like.*

This applicant shows she's proactive when she says she would try to work out her differences with her coworker, but realistic when she says that if she can't, she will find something to respect about her coworker—everyone has redeeming qualities.

 As a supervisor, what do you do when employees working under you don't get along?

*How to **answer** it: I actually encountered this situation a few months ago. There were two employees in my department who were both very nice people, but they got off on the wrong foot when one of them transferred into the department. I called a meeting with them and asked them to try to resolve their differences for the good of the department. I can't actually say they like each other now, but there is a level of respect between them.*

Nothing is better than a real-life experience. This job candidate was lucky enough to have one he could draw upon. He solved this problem in a very logical way, and was very honest about the outcome.

 What would you do if you disagreed with your boss?

*How to **answer** it: It would depend on the situation. If I disagreed with her about whether the office is warm or cold, I might not say anything. However, if I disagreed with my boss about whether the new marketing campaign was going to work, I'd share my thoughts with her.*

This applicant knows he has to choose his battles wisely. There's a difference between being disagreeable and disagreeing.

 What do you expect someone you supervise to do if she disagrees with you?

*How to **answer** it: I would expect that person to let me know what she's thinking. It could influence my decision. If she*

doesn't share her thoughts with me, I won't have the opportunity to hear her take on things.

This job candidate respects her coworkers' opinions. She knows it wouldn't be wise to make decisions without taking their comments into consideration.

Q: Have you ever been in a situation where the majority disagrees with you? What did you do?

*How to **answer** it: I haven't been in that situation, but here's what I would do if I were: First I would listen to why the majority felt the way they did. Then I'd have to decide whether I needed to reconsider my position. If I still felt strongly about it after hearing their side, I would try to persuade them.*

This candidate knew better than to dismiss the question just because he couldn't draw on his experience to answer it. Rather than make something up, he tells the interviewer what he would do if he were in that situation. His answer shows that he is flexible enough to try to see things differently, but strong enough in his convictions to not automatically go with the crowd.

Q: Tell me about a time when you had to defend an idea to your boss or someone else in an authoritative position.

*How to **answer** it: After working for my current employer for just a few months, I realized that many of our biggest accounts were not happy with the public relations services we were providing. It seemed that our Manhattan-based PR firm was having difficulty satisfying our West Coast clientele. As West Coast companies make up nearly 80 percent of our business, I approached my boss about changing PR firms. Because we had been using the same firm for nearly ten years, he was quite reluctant to change. When I showed him*

*the demographic shift in our customer base and had him
speak with several of our clients who had voiced concerns to
me in the past, he agreed that we might be better off switching agencies.*

The most important thing here is to make sure that you describe a
time or situation in which—after defending your idea—you were
able to see it through successfully. By explaining such a situation, you are telling the interviewer three important things about
yourself:

1. You have good ideas.
2. You will fight for what you believe in.
3. Those in higher positions respect your opinion and are willing to take a chance on your ideas.

Q: How did you get along with your last supervisor?

*How to **answer** it: We had a great relationship. I really
respected him, and I know he respected me, too. He knew he
could trust me with any project, so he always assigned me
those that were very challenging.*

This candidate describes his relationship with his boss on a professional level, and while doing that manages to say something very
positive about himself.

**Q: If you were unhappy with your job, how would you dis-
cuss this with your boss?**

*How to **answer** it: I've always had good relationships with
everyone I've worked for, so I think it would be to everyone's
benefit for me to be direct with my boss. First, I would make a
list of the things I'm unhappy with, as well as suggestions for
improving each situation. I would then ask for a meeting with*

my boss to go over the list point by point, being careful not to place any blame.

This interviewee smartly points out that she maintains good relationships with her bosses, which can withstand this type of discussion. She explains how she would be proactive in helping to find a solution for the problems she is dealing with at work.

What would your current coworkers say about you?

*How to **answer** it: My coworkers would say I'm very committed to my job. I work hard to contribute to each project's success, and I always share credit with everyone else who contributes to that success.*

This interviewee portrays himself as someone who is a team player. He sticks to talking about work-related matters.

What would you do about a long-term employee whose work has been slipping lately?

*How to **answer** it: I would talk to my employee to find out what was going on. Obviously if this person always did a good job, something must have happened to change that. As a supervisor, it is my job to find out what that is and help the employee fix the problem; it is also preferable to firing someone. It is generally more cost effective to retain a worker who already knows the job than to train someone new. It also is better for the morale of that person's coworkers, who don't want to see a coworker lose his job.*

This answer shows that the candidate has good managerial skills. While dismissing an unproductive employee may seem like a quick and easy solution in the short term, it can have a detrimental effect on the company in the end.

Q: **What do you do when you have a very unhappy customer?**

*How to **answer** it: My first step is to let the customer know I will listen to what he has to say. If the company has a strict policy regarding customer complaints, I will follow it. However, if I must use my own judgment, I will have to strike a balance between keeping the customer happy and not costing my employer too much. If I see that the customer's complaint is legitimate, I will do what it takes to remedy the situation.*

This applicant plays by the rules. He knows a satisfied customer will return, but he also realizes that a company is always concerned about its bottom line.

Q: **How are you at delegating?**

*How to **answer** it: I have such a high level of trust in my staff members that delegating to them is easy. I know each person's strengths and weaknesses, so I can easily decide who can handle what jobs and duties. I try to give people projects that challenge them but won't defeat them.*

This candidate is obviously a good manager. He puts a lot of thought into how to delegate responsibilities and makes a point of knowing his staff very well.

Creativity and Leadership Skills

Q: **What's the most innovative project you've ever worked on?**

*How **answer** it: When I worked with JLM Company last summer, I noticed that when sales inquiries would come into the office, they would be distributed haphazardly amongst the* *marketing assistants. Realizing that there had to be a better, more efficient way of logging these inquiries, I took it upon myself to set up a system. I organized these inquiries according to region and distributed them to the marketing assistants based on their regions. This approach enabled our marketing team to come up with better and more creative solutions to our sales problems, and it also addressed the specific concerns of our pre-existing customers.*

Give examples of your initiative and willingness to contribute new ideas. Discuss how your leadership skills have helped you accomplish your goals. Give a specific example that shows a creative, new, or unusual approach you took to reaching your goals.

Q: Describe a time when you've been able to overcome an obstacle in a creative manner.

*How to **answer** it: For months, the publishing company I worked for had been trying to get an appointment with a particular Fortune 500 company to talk about a possible advertising campaign. After several sales representatives tried to no avail, I volunteered to take a crack at the task. Rather than contact the vice president of advertising himself, I decided to target his assistant. I was able to schedule an appointment with the assistant and give her my sales pitch instead. I must have made quite an impression, because the assistant immediately scheduled me for a meeting with the VP for that very day. Two weeks later, we got the order, and the deal was made.*

A smart way to answer this question is to focus on how you overcome problems with the help and support of your coworkers. Show that in addition to being a creatively independent thinker, you are concerned about the company and your team as a whole. Also, illustrate your strength as a leader. Think about how you have approached a problem differently from how others might approach it, and how you have achieved success in doing so. Emphasize your creative solution along with its positive results.

Q: How resourceful are you?

How to answer it: I consider myself to be extremely resourceful. While product launches at my current company are generally the domain of our chief engineer, the CEO decided to let me conduct one, as I had shown much creativity in other projects. While the chief engineer usually would simply send out a press release describing the new product's virtues, I decided it was time for a change. I contacted three of our largest customers and asked them to try out the new product and let me know what they thought. With an overwhelmingly positive response to the new line, I then asked permission to videotape these real-life testimonials. The customers agreed, and rather than send out just a press release, we were able to create a podcast. The result was a far higher level of credibility for the company and product, and we exceeded our six-month sales quota. Personal endorsements have now become a cornerstone of all of our marketing campaigns.

This question specifically targets the candidate's level of creativity and initiative. Your best bet is to provide an example of how you've altered the traditional way of doing things at some point and attained the same—if not better—results. Focus on how you obtained crucial information or how you changed your personal style to get someone to cooperate. As always, make sure to sound confident without being cocky, and don't exaggerate the situation just to have a great answer to the question. Employers will find out if you are lying; if you are, you can rest assured you will not be hired.

Q: Describe an improvement you personally initiated.

How to answer it: When I began working for my previous employer, one of my duties was to send out customer satisfaction surveys. This was done as a traditional paper process which seemed cumbersome to me, especially since we had client e-mails in our database. I worked with one of the members of the tech team to create an online survey, which was sent directly to the customer's e-mail within ten days of the transaction. This new system saved time, money, and print resources, and it also increased overall customer survey response by 34 percent.

Here's your chance to prove your dedication to your work and your ability to see the entire picture. Show that, given the chance, you can be instrumental in making significant changes to the company or to the way things are done. Highlight your effectiveness in making things happen; express your desire to do the same for this company. Sometimes this same question can be asked in a more specific way. For example, describe a time when you thought an existing process or manner of doing things could have been done better, and what you did about it.

Q: **How would you describe your own personal management style?**

*How to **answer** it: Rather than tell someone what to do or answer a question directly, I try to encourage my employees to help find the solution. For example, if asked a question about how to proceed on a project or task, I will prompt the person to tell me what he thinks we should do. In addition to questions, I want to hear solutions. I like being able to lead my team, but I want to know that they are working to help solve problems as well. I like to think that by involving my staff in questions and problems that arise in the department, I am teaching them how to be effective leaders.*

Talk about your management style and interpersonal skills with your staff. Do you allow them to be creative or are you a take-charge sort of person? Think about how your staff views you. Are you a micromanager? Describe a particular skill you've learned from a leader you admire and discuss how you try to incorporate that into your own management style. Be careful that you portray yourself as a fair leader and not as a tyrant.

 Describe a time when you had to alter your leadership style.

How to **answer** *it: In my current position, I am put in charge of approximately one new project per month. Each month, I am assigned a new group of employees—usually a group of new recruits—to help them learn how to see a project through to completion. My usual style is to look the project over beforehand, figure out the best solution, and begin delegating tasks. About a year ago, the assigned group began to question my initial plan to complete the project. They proposed some alternate ideas, and I was quite impressed by their suggestions. While it had always been my style to assume that my idea was the right way to approach a project, this team taught me differently. Since then, the first step I take when beginning any new project is to talk with the group and figure out a solution—together.*

Assure the employer of your willingness and ability to create strong working relationships by making different kinds of people comfortable with your authority. Your answer should indicate a time when you encountered a person or group that questioned your leadership style, and you should illustrate how you worked to change it. Be specific. What initiatives did you take to improve a less-than-ideal situation? What would the other people involved say about you now? Don't make yourself out to be a tyrant, but don't seem like a wimp either. Indicate that the reasons for your change in style were a result of your keen ability to deal with people.

Q: How do you think a past subordinate would describe your leadership style?

*How to **answer** it: I think that people who have worked under me have considered it a positive experience. I look at my role as a supervisor as the chance to have a say in something and contribute to the success of the company. I do not believe it is my place to have the final ruling. I am not one of those people who constantly reminds you that I'm in charge. Before making decisions, I consult with my team to see what kinds of ideas they can come up with. This kind of leadership has been key to success in the past, and it's the model I plan to use throughout my career. Colleagues and employees have both commented to me on the positive work atmosphere that I create; I take that as the highest compliment.*

By asking this question, the interviewer is trying to determine what your references would say about you. When describing yourself, be objective and realistic without embellishing—or being overly modest. Describe candidly your leadership style; give specific examples that reflect your personal approach. Even if your style is to retain control, what are its positive aspects? Keep in mind that the employer may very likely call your colleagues to find out the truth from them. Rather than make excuses for your style, explain your leadership approach and why it works. If you can, give examples of how this style has succeeded.

Q: Do you believe that past job appraisals have adequately reflected your abilities as a leader?

*How to **answer** it: I think that the many goals I have surpassed and the various projects I have seen through to successful completion are proof of my strong leadership skills. I am sure that any job appraisal would mention how I look to my team for support, as well as how I take the time to clearly define our objectives to all those around me. By creating a* *certain amount of camaraderie, I have gained the confidence and respect of my coworkers, which, in my opinion, is the real key to success.*

If you've ever had an experience where—under your supervision—a project failed, this is the time to explain that struggle. Even if a project failed, how did you work to affect this project in a positive manner? What were the steps that you took to ensure its success anyway? Just because a project did not turn out as well as you had hoped does not mean that your job appraisal should be negative. Avoid taking offense at this question or blaming someone else. Regardless of your team, you were the leader. Talk about how you would translate your past successes and failures to this job. What lessons have you learned? Which pitfalls do you know to avoid in the future?

Q: Describe the situations in which you feel most comfortable as a leader.

How to answer it: I think that one of my talents is the ability to take complex issues and break them down. For this reason, I have always been very good at solving problems that involve facts and figures. As those who work around me are quite aware of this, they usually allow me to emerge as the leader in situations in which there is a complex problem; they look to me to find a solution and instruct them on how to proceed, and I am happy to do so. I am a highly effective leader in these situations. In situations in which there are political or emotional factors to consider, I usually prefer that someone else take the lead. In such situations, I simply resolve to be a good team player. In all other situations, I normally surface as a leader.

Your answer to this question says an awful lot about you. Do you feel comfortable leading a situation only when it is specifically asked of you, or do you assert yourself in situations in which you think your expertise could help bring a project to a successful conclusion? Talk about the projects you have led and how other people have trusted you. Why do you think people are willing to follow you in situations such as these? The best way to answer this question is to discuss instances when you were recognized as the leader because of your expertise in something, not because you were appointed project leader. If you're asked to describe situations in which you are a better contributor than leader, you can define types of problems that you're less comfortable working on or situations in which you feel you're too opinionated or biased to lead without controlling the group unfairly. Then end by describing instances when you've played the leader well.

Q: **Describe how comfortable you are working with people of higher rank versus working with employees of lower rank.**

*How to **answer** it: I am on a friendly basis with just about everyone I come into contact with throughout the course of my workday. I recently learned that one of the receptionists and I work out at the same gym, so we carpool after work and are becoming friends because of that. On the other hand, the general manager and I also share several common interests. We have golfed together on a few occasions and have spent many a lunch discussing our various common interests. I pride myself on getting to know those around me personally while, at the same time, building strong working relationships.*

Be very specific here in discussing your relationships. Talk about how you have been able to build strong relationships with all those around you. Don't talk as if those who work under you are below you socially, and don't seem too obsequious when talking about your boss. Those of higher rank should always command respect, but you shouldn't let them walk all over you. By discussing all the ways you help out your boss, you may be setting yourself up as the company's next doormat.

Problem-Solving Ability

Q: How do you usually go about solving a problem?

*How to **answer** it: The first step I take is to figure out all the possible causes for the problem. I then think about the outcomes that could arise from my taking action; I consider the best and worst case scenarios as well as the things that are likely to occur. I then try to relate this problem—and its possible causes—to a larger problem. When I have everything laid out in front of me, it is much easier to make a logical connection between cause and effect, and I can come up with a practical way of resolving the issue.*

The key here is to show the interviewer your initiative and your ability to make logical decisions. Convince the interviewer that you are able to solve a problem successfully and that you already have a set plan for tackling such complex issues. What criteria do you base your decisions on? Do others seem to have faith in your problem-solving abilities? If you can, give specific examples of times when you were able to use these problem-solving abilities to a successful conclusion.

Q: Describe a time when you've used a problem-solving process to obtain successful results.

*How to **answer** it: The hotel chain that I work for offers a free night's stay to any customer who has had an unpleasant experience there in the past. As customer service is a top priority of mine, I took it upon myself to follow up with some of the unsatisfied customers. Upon retrieving the names of all those customers who had complained about our hotels in the past few* *years, I noticed that several customers were arranging hotel stays around the country through abuse of this policy. I suggested that we set up a flagging program in our computer that would allow the clerk or person making reservations to recognize this customer as someone who had complained in the past.*

Hotel employees were instructed to make mention of this customer's past experience by stating something as simple as "Mr. Smith, I know that you have had an unpleasant experience with our hotel in the past, and I am happy that you have decided to give us a second chance. If there is anything I can do to make your stay more accommodating, please don't hesitate to contact me." For the customers who have had legitimate complaints in the past, this tactic allows us to be able to address their concerns more closely and make them aware that we are working to correct any problems they have found. Those customers who chose to abuse our satisfaction guaranteed policy are warned that their name is on record as having complained in the past, making it less likely that they will do so again after this stay. Because of this new system, our satisfaction rate has improved tremendously, and fraudulent cases have decreased.

You are trying to establish yourself as a fair employee who uses logic to solve difficult problems. When choosing a situation to describe, make sure it defines a real problem and a good solution that has helped in solving this issue. Describe, step by step, how the process you came up with was able to lead to a successful conclusion. What measures or benchmarks did you use to control or manage the process? What were the results?

Q: Tell me about a time when a problem that you failed to anticipate arose.

*How to **answer** it: My boss had asked me to spend a little time trying to find some inventive ways to cut costs in my department. I immediately got to work and found all sorts of* *ways to cut barely noticeable amounts of money in various areas that would result in an overall 10 percent decrease in costs. What I hadn't realized is that each of the department heads had already been asked to choose one area in which they would be willing to cut costs. The department heads responded that there was no area within their department that they were willing or able to cut any costs. Soon after I submitted my solution to my boss, I noticed the apathetic way in which each of the department heads dealt with me. I failed to realize that my solution had already been attempted and that there were a lot of negative feelings associated with my findings.*

Everyone has failed to anticipate a problem at some time, even the interviewer. The question is whether you're secure enough to 'fess up to it and see it as a learning experience. Discuss an incident in which you failed to see the warning signs that a problem was likely to occur. What did you learn from this experience? How has your judgment changed because of that incident?

Q: **Describe a time when a problem wasn't resolved to your satisfaction.**

*How to **answer** it: During last year's holiday season, we weren't able to complete a customer's order in time. Our production capacity was not sufficient to deliver the entire order on time. As a result, the customer asked for a discount on her order. I was upset by the fact that we did not take initiative and offer the customer a discount at the same time we informed her that her order would not be ready. The sense of goodwill and genuine regret for not having the order ready would have been greater.*

This question focuses on the candidate's standards of quality. Do you let things slide by when there is an easier or better way to solve the problem, or do you work tirelessly to ensure a satisfactory ending? Describe a situation in which you foresaw long-term complications from a problem that was poorly handled. Did you initiate the resolution of this situation? If the solution still wasn't satisfactory, did you do anything else? If there was nothing else you could do, why not?

Q: **Describe an opportunity in which you felt the risks far outweighed the rewards.**

*How to **answer** it:* We were given the opportunity to purchase manufacturing equipment at thirty cents on the dollar from a company that had recently dissolved. At the time, we anticipated an overhaul of our manufacturing facility five years down the road. I made the decision that it was too far into the future to spend money only to have idle capacity for a five-year period. If market conditions had shown more promise for new sales in the initial two-year period, I would have gone ahead with it.

The interviewer wants to be assured that the candidate is able to take reasonable risks without being foolish. The best way to answer this question is to offer an example of a time when you were given a decision to make and were able to use good judgment in determining the risks versus the benefits. How was the outcome of your decision preferable to what might have happened? Were you aware of the possible risks? What was the thought process you used to decide against this?

Personal Questions

Q: **Tell me about yourself.**

*How to **answer** it:* I attended Ace Business College, where I earned my associate's degree in office technology five years ago. I started working as a library clerk right after

I graduated, and after a year I was promoted to assistant circulation manager. I helped the library switch over to a new circulation system about two years ago. I was part of the team that selected the new system, and I helped train our department in its use. In addition to my technical skills, I am adept at troubleshooting. I also work well with customers, helping to solve any problems that arise. I'm now ready to take on a job with more responsibility, and I know I will make a great circulation manager.

This candidate tells the interviewer about his skills and experience and shows why he is qualified for the job. He doesn't wander off course, revealing information that is irrelevant. The answer is relatively short and, more importantly, to the point.

 **What do you consider to be your biggest weakness?**

*How to **answer** it: I am very dedicated to my job, and I expect the same level of dedication from other people. Not everyone feels the same way about work and sometimes my expectations are too high.*

Wouldn't every boss love such a dedicated employee? This interviewee knew she had to find a weakness that her prospective employer would see as a strength. Another option is to pick a weakness that is somewhat innocuous.

*How to **answer** it: I give myself a quick pat on the back and move on to the next project. Of course, I take the time to figure out what helped me succeed and use that experience to help me the next time.*

This prospective employee takes appropriate pride in her success, while ascribing to the old adage "Don't rest on your laurels." She also learns from her experience.

How do you handle failure?

*How to **answer** it: I give myself a short time to feel sad, but I don't dwell on it. Without spending too much energy on it, I always try to figure out where things went wrong. If I don't do that, I won't know what I need to do to succeed next time.*

This isn't someone who wastes any time feeling sorry for himself. He's also smart enough to learn from his mistakes.

 Do you prefer to work alone or as part of a team?

*How to **answer** it: Each situation is different. Having a team to collaborate with works better for some projects, while it's best for one person to work on other projects. I enjoy being part of a team, but I can work independently, too.*

This interviewer shows that she's flexible and can adapt to working in either situation.

 What do you consider to be your greatest strength?

*How to **answer** it: My greatest strength is my ability to see a project through from its inception to its completion. Each project I am assigned is important to me, and I always make sure it gets the appropriate amount of attention.*

Notice the interviewee said each project gets the "appropriate amount of attention" and not "all my attention." She clearly knows that not all projects need the same amount of attention and indicates that she knows how to prioritize.

Do you like to take risks or are you cautious?

*How to **answer** it: I'll take risks, but I always proceed with caution, so I guess I fall somewhere in between. I like to see what my odds are before I take a risk. I also want to know what I stand to gain or lose.*

This candidate is a careful decision-maker who isn't afraid to take risks if there is a high probability of success. He also wants to make sure the risk is worth taking. He's not a gambler, but he's not afraid to take chances when it's appropriate to do so.

 We're not one of those companies that do things the same way year after year. How do you react to change?

*How to **answer** it: When appropriate, change is important. For example, when I heard about a new payroll system at a conference last year, I did a little investigating, found out it was better than what we were using, and recommended we move over to it.*

This interviewee has shown that she doesn't shy away from change, even providing a good example of how she initiated it at work. She has also shown that she doesn't jump into change just for the sake of doing something different, but rather, does her homework first.

 How do you make decisions?

*How to **answer** it: I evaluate the situation before I decide what I need to do. If there is someone who has had experience with similar situations, I'm not afraid to ask for advice.*

This interviewee isn't going to make a decision without considering it carefully. She is also very resourceful; seeking advice from people with more experience is always a good idea.

 Can you describe your ideal work environment?

*How to **answer** it: I want to work in an environment where I can use my presentation skills to help the company increase its client roster. It's important that I work in a fast-paced environment because I like being busy. I want to work somewhere where employees are recognized for their contributions.*

Based on some research, she is able to describe both the job that she's interviewing for and her potential employer. By showing that her ideal fits with what the job requires, she shows that she is the perfect fit for the position.

How do you explain your success in the workplace?

How to answer it: In this age of technology, human contact is highly underrated. I know how frustrated I get when I call a company and am met with a barrage of computer voices telling me which number to hit and whom to call. In business, I never assume that a customer is satisfied until she has told me so directly. I take a very personal approach to following up with every customer. The feedback that I have received—both positive and negative—has provided valuable insight into the quality and characteristics of our products. What augments my past successes even more is how much the customer appreciates these follow-ups, especially when there's been some sort of problem and I still have the opportunity to correct it on a timely basis. And the customer feedback doesn't just benefit me; I'm always passing on customer comments to our production and design teams so that we can ensure we are making the best possible product.

Again, the key to answering such personal questions is to be honest but not arrogant. You should not be embarrassed to toot your own horn a little. If you've accomplished something in the workplace (or anywhere else), don't be afraid to talk about it. It's not enough for you to tell the interviewer how great you are. You have to show him specific examples. Discuss the steps you've taken to ensure that you are considered a worthwhile employee, and mention that little bit extra that you do. Talk about observations other people have made about your strengths or talents. This question is similar to the question, What sets you apart from the crowd?

KEY WORDS AND PHRASES

Important skills
Advanced capabilities
The skills you are seeking
Specific examples
Ever-changing technology
Latest marketing trends
Creativity
New ideas
Important role of the web
I'd like to gain more experience.
I'd like to help.
I'd want the opportunity to move up.
I want to develop negotiating skills.
This job will offer me opportunities.
I want to acquire the necessary skills.
I've made an effort to develop these skills.
I consider myself well versed.
I am a professional.
I do a lot of research.
Very organized
Work well on a team
Have great communication skills
I found someone to fix the problem.
I prioritize my work.
Figure out what needs to get done first
Have formal and informal experience
Primary responsibility
Ability to create deeper relationships
My favorite type of coworker
Confidence is always important.

Focus on the positive
Share my thoughts
I would listen.
I would try to persuade.
Respect
Had good relations with those I worked for
Careful not to place blame
Very committed
Talk to my employees
Help employees fix problems
Listen to what others have to say
Do what it takes
Remedy the situation
Know everyone's strengths and weaknesses
Decide who can handle what
Give people projects that challenge them
Set up systems
Schedule
Extremely resourceful
Exceed my quota
Create surveys
Encourage employees to help find solutions
Delegate tasks
Consult with my team
I create a positive work atmosphere.
Goals I've surpassed
Successfully complete
Strong leadership skills
Create camaraderie
Solve problems
I'm a good team player.
Build strong working relationships
Figure out the causes of a problem

Make connections between cause and effect
Address customer concerns
Improve satisfaction rates
Find ways to cut costs
Help train others
Work well with customers
Take on jobs with more responsibility
I'm dedicated to my job.
I set high expectations for myself.
I enjoy being part of a team.
I can work independently.
See a project through
Take risks when appropriate
Change is important
I'm not afraid to ask for advice.
Fast-paced environment
I like being busy.
Take a personal approach

Chapter 3

Describing
Your
Achievements

WHEN YOU GO IN FOR A JOB INTERVIEW, ALONG WITH LEARNING ABOUT YOUR personality and skills, the prospective employer will be very interested in learning about your accomplishments. Your accomplishments give him insight into what you are capable of doing for him and his company. An accomplishment, also known as an achievement, can be defined as something that was successfully completed as a direct result of your efforts.

Prepare a list of your accomplishments prior to your job interview. The accomplishments you choose to highlight should demonstrate your skills and abilities. Remember to use examples of things that came about as a direct result of your efforts. The accomplishments you include on your list should be realistic and verifiable. That's not to say you should be modest on a job interview; go ahead and brag about yourself. However, don't consider stretching the truth—not even just a little. The interviewer may be suspicious of something that sounds too good to be true, and if she tries to verify something you told her and cannot, it will certainly reflect poorly on you.

Try to quantify your accomplishments when possible. Use actual numbers or percentages when you are discussing anything that can be expressed in quantifiable terms, such as increases in profits or decreases in costs. Being able to say that you increased sales by 20 percent or cut your department's costs by 35 percent is much better than saying "I increased sales a lot" or "I cut costs greatly."

When deciding which achievements to discuss on an interview, always remember to choose the ones that best demonstrate your ability to do the job you are interviewing for. Highlight skills that you think the prospective employer is looking for in a new employee. The best thing about accomplishments is that they can be examples from your professional career, academic years, or personal experiences. Use the following examples to highlight your achievements.

Professional and Personal Accomplishments

 Tell me about a major accomplishment in your life.

*How to **answer** it: As the publicity director of a tiny, alternative publishing house, it can be difficult to get major sources to review our books. Because the subjects we cover are often far from the mainstream, many television shows and review publications find our topics a bit too controversial. Last year, we published a book that I really thought could be a number one bestseller. Though I always put forth a lot of effort to publicize all of the books we published, I was particularly interested in seeing this little gem find its way from obscurity to popularity. Because of my efforts, coverage of this book was astronomical, and the book became a New York Times bestseller, with both the author and the book becoming household names.*

Talk to the interviewer about an accomplishment in your life that you are most proud of. The accomplishment should be work related, but it doesn't have to be. Be honest and be specific. Don't just throw out a general statement ("I won an award"); describe the steps you took to accomplish this goal and how all your hard work paid off in the end. One job seeker brought along a picture of herself receiving a prestigious award from a well-known celebrity at an industry awards dinner. It stimulated conversation and made an impression on the interviewer, who would be likely to remember the candidate after the interview was over. Don't stretch the truth, as interviewers have ways of finding out whether your story is true. Don't be long winded; instead, focus on your actual accomplishments and the steps leading up to them. The interviewer wants to know whether you will be able to contribute something to this company; this is a great opportunity to prove that you can.

Q: Tell me about a project you completed ahead of schedule.

*How to **answer** it: I was in charge of a new product rollout. In general we completed each phase without a major setback—which was partially luck—but I also systematically called two days ahead of every deadline to check the status with all groups involved. I believe that is what made the real difference. The launch took place two weeks ahead of plan—a very significant period of time in our industry, where shelf life for products is generally less than one year.*

In discussing how you were able to complete a project ahead of schedule, make sure that you are not forcing the interviewer to question the integrity of the project, or the attention to detail you displayed while working on it. Focus on how you set goals and schedules, measured results, and championed the outcome of a project. This question is aimed at your diligence in accomplishing tasks and, assuming the project required group effort, at your leadership skills.

Q: **Can you tell me about your greatest accomplishment at work?**

*How to **answer** it: I'm particularly proud of the mentoring program I started about five years ago. I noticed that new employees were having trouble getting acclimated to the company, causing a very high turnover rate during the first year of employment. I developed a program that allowed us to assign each new employee to an employee who had been with the company for at least three years. This allowed new hires to make a smoother transition. Now, 90 percent of new employees are still with us after their one-year anniversaries, up from 50 percent before we started the mentorship program.*

The interviewee provides a specific example in response to this question. She also highlights the fact that she took initiative in developing it; she saw a problem and found a solution. She also shows the result of her efforts with actual numbers.

Q: **Describe how you accomplished a work-related goal.**

*How to **answer** it: When I started working for Daylight Publications, I discovered that I had inherited a huge file cabinet full of photographs. We used photographs in our magazine but usually wound up purchasing stock photos, because our own collection was so disorganized it was impossible to find anything. I designed a filing system and set about putting things in order. I set aside fifteen minutes each day and was able to work my way through the whole collection in about seven months.*

This answer demonstrates how the interviewee took the initiative to set a goal in order to save her employer money. She then talks about how she went about reaching that goal by using her organization and time management skills.

Q: **Can you describe how you accomplished a personal goal?**

How to answer it: I wrote a short story and my goal was to get it published. I went to the library and researched which magazines accepted short story submissions. Then I sent my story to the magazines that published stories in the same genre as mine. My story was accepted by one of them and was finally published a little over a year ago.

This candidate talks about the steps he took to reach his personal goal. He used his research skills to find out where to send his story.

Q: **What has been your greatest accomplishment as part of a team?**

How to answer it: I worked on a team that developed a program for children who were going home to an empty house after school because their parents worked. We had volunteers who would help the kids with their homework and give them time to just burn off energy after sitting in a classroom all day. By the time we actually opened the center, we had seventy-five children enrolled. That told us we were providing a service that was clearly needed.

This candidate describes in detail the project she considers her greatest accomplishment as part of a team. She talks about what was needed, what they did to fill that need, and what the end result was.

Q: **Name the two work-related accomplishments that you are the proudest of.**

How to answer it: I converted a manual payroll system to a computerized system, which cut down the amount of time we spent on payroll each week. I wrote a manual that explained all bookkeeping department procedures in our company. New employees receive a copy of this manual, which helps them learn their job faster.

Each of the accomplishments this candidate discusses has had a positive result on the company and highlights his many skills.

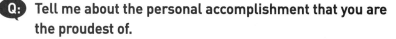 **Tell me about the personal accomplishment that you are the proudest of.**

How to answer it: Last year I ran a marathon for the first time. I've been a runner for years, but I never ran more than four miles at a time. I began training four months before the big day. It was hard, but I kept going and I ended up finishing in just over four hours, which I've heard is pretty good for a first-time marathoner.

By discussing running a marathon, this candidate demonstrates that she will work hard to reach her goals. She also shows that she is not afraid of a challenge, something her prospective employer should appreciate.

What accomplishments have you made so far in reaching your long-range goals?

How to answer it: My long-range goal is to be a school principal. I've been teaching for ten years, first at PS 118 and then at PS 114. After five years of teaching second grade at PS 114, I was asked to be grade leader. My experience working with faculty and developing new programs for students has prepared me for the position of assistant principal. I look forward to using my skills to work on some of the projects we discussed earlier.

This candidate has demonstrated how he has taken steps to reach his goal and plans to continue to do so. He also makes a point of talking about the contributions he plans to make in the job that he's interviewing for.

 What motivates you to go above and beyond the call of duty?

*How to **answer** it:* Honestly, I don't have a sense of what is above and beyond the call of duty. It's not like I can just do enough to get by and then stop. When I work on a project, I do my very best, always.

This statement shows that this job candidate is truly a hard worker who cares about her work. It's more than just a job to her. She can't justify giving less than her best effort to any project entrusted to her.

 Have you ever been asked to take on a project because of your unique skill or ability?

*How to **answer** it:* Our senior developer regularly asks me to troubleshoot new programs. I've been very successful at figuring out why programs aren't working properly, and I can usually do it pretty quickly, allowing the team to move forward.

This candidate chose to talk about a skill that will be as valuable to his prospective employer as it is to his current one.

Contributions You've Made

 Tell me about a contribution you've made to a team accomplishment.

*How to **answer** it:* In my current company, all projects are group projects. My last work group was made up of five very intelligent and very creative people. However, the overall technical skills were a bit lacking. People knew how they wanted our presentation to look, but they didn't know how to go about *achieving it. I am an avid computer user and have taken several classes in graphic design. I think our group's final product was a good mix of creativity and technology. I used my computer skills to help our team come up with a fantastic presentation that the client accepted without hesitation.*

Even if you spend most of your time working independently—or work independently because you choose to—the interviewer wants to be reassured that you deal with other people well. When placed within a group setting, do you immediately try to take control or do you offer up a certain expertise? Think about the kinds of tasks you've performed before in group settings, and the skills that you have mastered. What would the other members of your team say about your contributions? Would they want to work with you again? Would they consider your skills vital to the team's success? Offer proof, using specific examples, that you delivered more than the team expected and that the team would compliment your contributions to the group's efforts.

Q: Are there any special contributions you feel you've made to your employer?

*How to **answer** it: For the past four years, I have run a Walk for Hunger campaign at my company as part of our corporate social responsibility program. I believe that it is a very important cause, and I know it can be difficult for a company to find volunteers, so I stepped in to help. Each year has been more successful than the last, and coworkers have told me it's one of the things they look forward to most throughout the course of the year, which obviously makes me very happy.*

Convince the interviewer that you are ready to go the extra mile for your employer. Tell her about a specific time when you delivered more than the employer expected. If you were hired, what situations would you handle especially well? What unique contributions can you make to the organization? How would you go the extra mile?

 Tell me about a quantifiable outcome of one of your efforts.

*How to **answer** it: I reorganized inventory planning and was able to automate the inventory-recorder function. A task that used to take forty hours to complete now only takes five!*

One truth—in business, especially—is that numbers don't lie. One of the easiest ways to showcase your accomplishments is to quantify them. But remember, unless you're talking about sales dollars or company profits, don't talk dollar amounts or the earnings of colleagues. Describe a specific accomplishment that produced a clear benefit. Offer proof, using real examples, that you deliver more than what's expected.

 Tell me how you were of value to your previous employer.

*How to **answer** it: My previous employer valued my ability to deal with difficult clients. Whenever we had a client who was very demanding, my boss would ask me to be the one to work with him. She said she knew I was so levelheaded that I would always stay calm, even when a client was really trying my patience.*

With this answer the candidate not only says why he thinks his boss values him, he talks about it from her perspective. He presents a skill that will be valuable to this employer as well.

 Have you ever had to take over an assignment at the last minute?

*How to **answer** it: I've had to do that more than once— actually several times. The most recent was when a colleague*

was scheduled to attend a meeting out of town and came down with the flu two days before he was supposed to leave. My boss asked me if I could attend the meeting and make the presentation my colleague was supposed to make. I had two days to learn everything about the project. I went over pages and pages of notes and put together a presentation of my own, incorporating input from my colleague, who I spoke to on the phone several times a day.

Not only does this interviewee say he has taken over an assignment at the last minute, he talks about a specific case. He shows how he stepped in and learned what he needed to learn to make a successful presentation.

Q: **If I asked your current employer to tell me about your accomplishments, what do you think she would say?**

How to answer it: She would probably talk about the time she asked me to present a new marketing campaign to one of our more difficult clients. I spent over a week preparing for that presentation. Since I knew this client was hard to please, I had to make sure I anticipated every objection he might have. He actually loved the presentation, and the campaign increased sales by 50 percent.

This question gives the candidate a chance to talk about an accomplishment he is proud of. He talks about anticipating possible difficulties and the end result, an increase in sales.

Q: **If I asked a college professor about one of your accomplishments, what would he or she say?**

How to answer it: I worked on a major research project under the supervision of my psychology professor. We collected data over the course of a year and after analyzing the data, we wrote up the results as an article that we submitted to the Journal of Kangaroo Psychology. It was accepted, and it was published a month before I graduated.

This candidate chose to talk about something that had a tangible result—publication in a professional journal.

Q: **Have you ever come up with new ways to solve a problem?**

*How to **answer** it: Yes, I have. We had a problem with dismissal from our after-school program. Too many children were leaving at once, causing a bit of chaos in our parking lot. I developed a system for releasing children alphabetically so that parents could pick up siblings in different grades at the same time. If we had released children by grade, parents would have had to wait around for children who were in different grade levels. That would have added to the chaos.*

The candidate states a specific problem and then discusses the steps she took to solve it. She even mentions how she anticipated and then prevented a potential problem.

Q: **What situations do your colleagues rely on you to handle?**

*How to **answer** it: Whenever we're faced with a difficult or dissatisfied client, my coworkers come to me. Unlike some of my coworkers, I never lose my temper in front of customers. My ability to remain objective has proven extremely important, especially when dealing with an irate client.*

Even within a strictly team setting, there are obviously situations that you are better at handling than your colleagues are. Even though you may not be singled out to deal with each of these situations, tell the interviewer about the situations that you excel in. Which situations are you more qualified for (or better at handling) than your peers? This question provides a good opportunity for you to showcase your dependability, strength of character, and professionalism.

Q: Have you ever "saved the day" for your employer?

How to answer it: Yes, I have. It was the afternoon before our company was hosting a big luncheon. We called the caterer to confirm some of the details, but her number had been disconnected. We found out she had gone out of business and didn't bother to let us know. I called some friends at other companies and got a list of caterers together, called them, and got someone to do the job. My boss couldn't believe I managed to hire someone on such short notice.

The interviewee, by giving this example, shows how her resourcefulness helped her solve her employer's problem.

Q: Have you ever done something that directly helped your employer either increase profits or decrease costs?

How to answer it: I recently found a way to help my employer save money on office supplies. For years, they bought office supplies from the same place. It was several blocks away, so it was pretty convenient. I have found that shopping online is almost always less expensive than shopping in a store, so I did a little comparison shopping and I found an online source for our office supplies at a savings of 40 percent from what we were paying for the same items. Plus, the items are delivered, which is even more convenient. As long as we order several items at once, delivery is free.

This interviewee's answer illustrates how she looks out for her employer's best interests.

Challenges You've Overcome

Q: **Tell me about an accomplishment you had a difficult time achieving.**

*How to **answer** it:* Years ago, when I first began working for my current company, part of my job required meeting with our technical support staff once a week to find out about any technical problems or issues we faced. As part of the human resources team, it was my duty to voice any concerns to the right people and get the problems fixed. I didn't have very much experience with computers. For the most part, I didn't understand their complaints. Back then, I didn't even know what a modem was, and I certainly didn't know how to increase the speed of one.

I decided that to do a great job, I would need to learn more about what it was that each of our departments did. Whenever I could find the time, I would go down to the technical department and sit in for a while. When I had questions, I would ask them. The staff was always very happy to answer and seemed pleased that I had taken so much interest in learning more about their job. Although I definitely struggled for the first month or so, I now make a consistent effort to keep pace with new technology because I have seen first hand how it impacts employee satisfaction and overall productivity.

Be careful what you are implying when you answer this question. Citing an instance in which the problem was a coworker can make you sound as though you're not much of a team player, a bit of a know-it-all, or worse, a dinosaur who won't change with the times. Talk to the interviewer about a time when you accomplished something despite obstacles, lack of training, or inadequate experience. Focus on your ability to overcome this problem and achieve successful results. Express your willingness to accept challenges and triumph over them.

Q: **Tell me about something you accomplished that required strict discipline.**

How to ***answer*** *it: When I was a full-time graduate student, my one goal was to avoid accruing any more student loan debt. In addition to working toward an advanced degree in journalism, I spent twenty hours a week as an intern at a local magazine and another twenty-five hours a week as a waitress. Juggling these three hectic, very demanding schedules was certainly a challenge, but it makes me appreciate all that I have achieved.*

Here's another opportunity for you to discuss a skill you have had to work hard to develop and have been successful doing. This is also an opportunity to discuss a time when the amount of work you had and the time you needed to finish it were a challenge. Discuss your strong time management skills and how you are able to prioritize to accomplish your goal. How did you remain focused? What were the results? What did you learn from the experience?

Q: **Tell me about the most difficult work or personal experience you've ever had to face.**

How to ***answer*** *it: A coworker with whom I was very close was going through a very difficult time and had begun to abuse drugs and alcohol. With our firm's support, he decided that the best thing for him was to attend a rehabilitation center. For the next six months, I had to take on much of this person's work in addition to my own. While the long hours and added pressure were not the ideal situation, I know that he would have done the same for me, so I never once regretted my decision. It's very important to me to have that kind of trust among the members of my work group, and I am glad that I was able to help a friend in need. It is certainly something I will always be proud of.*

The ultimate goal of this question is to find out how well you handle pressure. Ideally, you want to describe a situation—personal or professional—that involved a great deal of conflict and challenge and, as a result, placed you under an unusual amount of stress. Explain, specifically, what the problems were and what you did to resolve them. What was the result? Is it something you would do again?

Q: How have you handled criticism of your work in the past?

How to answer it: The first time I ever had a client complain to me, I was devastated. The client was upset about the downtime in ATM machines. Though her complaint had nothing to do with my professional service of the account, I did take it a bit personally. However, rather than dwell on my own disappointment, I began to work very closely with this client to see whether there was something I could do about her suggestion. While I couldn't change our ATM system, I was able to learn a lot from the experience. I learned that showing empathy usually calms an unpleasant situation. I also learned that no client is going to be happy with everything, even if that client's overall experience is positive. I know that I should not take things personally and, instead, focus on initiatives that will yield customer satisfaction without distracting from my core duties.

The interviewer is trying to learn something about your accountability and professional character. Talk about a time when you were engaged in a specific project or work habit that caused you a problem. Then discuss how you finally faced up to the problem and overcame it. Alternatively, you might describe a time you responded objectively and professionally to particularly harsh or unreasonable criticism of your work. In either case, finish the comment by talking about what you learned from this experience. Remember: Always keep things positive, and refrain from complaining or slandering any past work associates.

Q: **Tell me about one of your projects that failed.**

How to answer it: I've always been somewhat of a worka-holic and have the attitude that I can tackle anything and achieve good results. After a rather destructive hurricane, my insurance company was inundated with claims. I really believed that I was completely capable of handling all the claims in my area and dove right into a series of eighteen-hour workdays. Even when others in the office would offer to help, I reassured them that I had it all under control. After about a week and a half, I realized that there was no way I could complete all of the claims on time and on my own. I had to begin delegating some of the responsibility to my investigators. What I learned was that no matter how efficient and competent you are, there are always situations in which you need to ask for help from others.

Make sure that you demonstrate the ability to be humble when answering this type of question. One of the worst answers you can come up with in a situation such as this one is "I can't think of anything I've ever failed at" or "I've never had a project that failed." Everyone has failed at one time or another, and it's okay to admit it. Show the employer how much you can learn from your mistakes. In hindsight, what do you think you could have and should have done differently? How have you altered your leadership or professional style as a result of this experience?

Q: **Tell me about a time when you had a real problem getting along with one of your work associates.**

How to answer it: I have always thought of myself as an easygoing person; I tend to get along with most people. However, I do remember one time when we brought in a new associate who was very bossy—bossy to the point where his attitude really offended one of our interns. As this was not the *type of management style that our employees were used to, I took it upon myself to pull the new associate aside and explain that I found it more productive to ask people for help than to give orders. Unfortunately, he seemed more offended by my concern for our employees and about the sour relationship he was beginning to form with them than pleased with or grateful for my attempt to help him. The advice didn't change anything with his attitude, but we were much more careful with our hiring process after that experience.*

The best way to answer this question is to discuss a difference in work ethic between you and an associate, not an all-out hatred for each other. Avoid discussing a personality clash between you and a coworker. Instead, speak about a situation with which the interviewer is likely to empathize. For example, you might describe someone whose standards of excellence were perhaps less stringent than yours. Be sure to talk about the steps you took to mend this problem and the end result was.

Q: **Have you ever had to work with a manager who you thought was unfair to you or who was just plain difficult to get along with?**

How to answer it: Fortunately, I've never really run into that problem. Of course, my current boss has to work under time constraints—just like everyone else—and she sometimes has a tendency to answer things rather bluntly to push our department to meet its goals. But I've never considered that unfair or hard to handle; it's just part of the job. My supervisors and I have always gotten along quite well.

Again, no matter how many times an interviewer gives you the opportunity to do so, never criticize a current or former employer! The interviewer is not really interested in finding out whether or not you have worked for difficult people in the past—we all have. What he is trying to discover is whether or not (and how easily) you are willing to badmouth these people.

Q: **How do you handle tension with your boss?**

How to **answer** *it: The only tension I've ever felt occurred only once, when we both got too busy to keep each other informed. My boss overcommitted me with a short deadline, not knowing I was bogged down with another client problem. I believe firmly in the importance of staff meetings to keep coworkers aware and respectful of the demands on each other's time, and I worked closely with my boss to develop a formalized meeting schedule.*

Though the question itself is set in the present tense, your best bet in answering it is to use the past tense. The safest ground here is to describe an example of a miscommunication in your early relationship with a boss and how you resolved it. Talk about the problem itself, but focus more on how the two of you handled the problem. Describe the steps you have taken since that incident to ensure that a similar problem does not reoccur.

Recognition and Rewards You've Received

Q: **Have you ever received formal recognition for something you accomplished?**

How to **answer** *it: Yes. I won Salesperson of the Month four times when I was working for Ace Stereo. Those with the largest increase in sales over the previous month were rewarded in this way.*

This candidate chose to discuss being rewarded for something that would be valued by any company—high sales volume.

Q: How has your employer rewarded your accomplishments?

*How to **answer** it: My employer initially rewarded me by trusting me enough to give me additional responsibility. This gave me a chance to prove myself, and I was ultimately rewarded with a big promotion.*

This candidate discusses how at first his reward was simply being asked to do more. Did he object to that? No. It only gave him the opportunity to further prove himself so that he received the reward of a promotion.

Q: You seem to have accomplished a lot in your current job. Do you know why you weren't promoted?

*How to **answer** it: I wasn't promoted because unfortunately there wasn't a position to promote me to. JFR was a very small family-owned firm. The boss's two sons held the top positions, which were right above my position.*

The candidate explains why he couldn't move beyond his current position in spite of his accomplishments. He doesn't seem resentful, but rather accepts this fact.

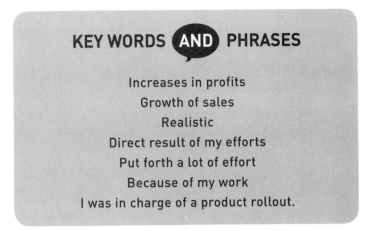

KEY WORDS AND PHRASES

Increases in profits
Growth of sales
Realistic
Direct result of my efforts
Put forth a lot of effort
Because of my work
I was in charge of a product rollout.

Ahead of schedule
I'm particularly proud of
I developed a program.
I designed a system.
Put things in order
Took the initiative
Set my goal
Worked on a team that developed a program
Service that was needed
Did what was necessary
Filled a need
I wrote a manual.
I kept going.
Not afraid of a challenge
My experience working with
I look forward to using my skills.
I always do my best.
Troubleshoot
Allow the team to move forward
Use my skills to help the team
Vital to the team's success
Volunteer
Go the extra mile
Reorganize
Benefit
I'm levelheaded.
I always stay calm.
Take over an assignment
Anticipate objections
Make suggestions of my own
Learn what I needed
Worked on a major project
I developed a system.

I prevented a potential problem.
I never lose my temper.
Remain objective
Resourcefulness
Comparison shopping
Decrease costs
Voice concerns
Fix problems
Look out for the employer's best interests
Juggle demanding schedules
Strong time management skills
Build trust among my group
Work closely with clients
Learn from the experience
Empathy
Accountability
Professional character
Situations in which you need help
Get along with people
Work ethic
Get along with supervisors
Importance of meetings
Worked closely with the boss
Rewarded
Praised
A chance to prove myself

Chapter 4

Explaining
Your Goals and
Interests

YOU PROBABLY HAVE A SENSE OF HOW YOU WANT YOUR CAREER TO PROGRESS. YOUR research into your chosen industry will show you what the typical progression is for someone in your chosen career path. Your interviewer will probably be interested to know what your goals are and how the job you are interviewing for fits into your long-term goals.

Where do you want to be two years from now? It's a question that relates specifically to your career goals, and you should make sure that your answer coincides with the typical career path you are about to embark on. If you are interviewing for the position of front desk clerk, for example, you should not tell the interviewer that in two years you hope to be running the company. Keep your goals realistic, and always make sure that—within the given time period you are asked about—they are attainable.

Though questions about personal interests are becoming less and less common (some can—inadvertently—lead to illegal information), you still may be asked about personal interests and hobbies. Why would an employer want to know how you spend your weekends? Finding out what you do in your leisure time is a good and quick way to get to know you as a person, not just a job applicant. Some questions that may go through an interviewer's mind while she asks you about your outside interests are whether you have a balanced lifestyle, whether your personality is reflected in the type of job you choose, and whether your personal and professional interests seem compatible.

Long- and Short-Term Goals

Q: **What are your long-term goals?**

*How to **answer** it: I want to move into a supervisory position eventually. I know that will take time and hard work, but it is something I expect to achieve.*

That's a good answer as long as the interviewer isn't the only supervisor. (The interviewee doesn't want to seem as if he's after the interviewer's job.) It's important to emphasize that you have goals—and also that you are willing to do the work to reach them.

Q: **What are your short-term goals?**

*How to **answer** it: I want to work for a company that is growing, in a position that allows me to use my skills to help that growth. I know your company is trying to expand into the teen market. My experience selling to that market will help your company reach its goals.*

This interviewee's goals are aligned with those of the company. By giving an example of how she will help the company meet its goals, she has forced the employer to visualize her as an employee. This answer also shows that the interviewee took the time to research the company before her appointment.

Q: **Do you consider yourself a leader?**

*How to **answer** it: I am willing to take on responsibility, I am persuasive, and I can delegate. All these qualities make me a* *good leader. If a situation calls for someone to take charge, I will certainly step forward.*

This interviewer states the qualities that make her a good leader but knows to tread lightly here. She wants to show she can evaluate the needs of each situation and step forward if necessary, while making it clear she's a team player.

Q: Are you a procrastinator or do you like to get things done?

*How to **answer** it: Though I've been known to procrastinate on occasion, I don't make a habit of it. When someone hands me a project that needs to be done in a timely fashion, I will get it done.*

Who hasn't procrastinated on occasion? What matters is that this candidate knows the difference between a project that can wait and one that needs to be done right away, and can finish the pressing ones in time to meet deadlines.

Q: I see that you worked full-time while attending graduate school. How did you manage to balance everything?

*How to **answer** it: It was difficult, but I managed not to fall behind at work or school. I worked five full days a week and took classes two evenings a week. I studied on the other three nights and on the weekends.*

This candidate shows that he was determined to complete his degree but not at the expense of his job.

Q: How do you want your career to progress in the next few years?

*How to **answer** it: Over the next few years, I would like to be at the point where I have bottom-line budget responsibility and* *charge of a production unit in which I have labor-relations, quality-control, design, and manufacturing responsibilities. I believe this job will go a long way toward helping me meet my career goals.*

Avoid the temptation to suggest job titles; this makes you seem unbending and unrealistic since you don't know or control the system of promotion. Likewise, you don't know how long it might have taken your interviewer to reach certain levels, and you wouldn't want to offend her. On the other hand, you don't want to be too general either. The best way to answer this question is to discuss the new experiences you would like to have in the next few years and the responsibilities you would like to acquire.

Q: **What new challenges would you enjoy taking on?**

*How to **answer** it: I've worked in various positions in the hospitality industry for more than eight years and have progressively worked in larger, more prestigious hotels. I've learned both the food and beverage side of the business as well as the hotel management side. Armed with that background, I now believe I'm ready to take part in the convention and conference area.*

Based on the skills you have learned and enjoyed using in your current position, describe the new challenges that you would like to take on and that you feel capable of handling. Be as specific as you can, considering what you know about the current or future direction of the position, department, and company as a whole. Think about the duties of the job at hand and which ones might provide you with a bit of a challenge.

Q: **What are your long-term career plans?**

*How to **answer** it: My long-term career goals are to become known as an industry expert and to have earned a respectable* *management position with responsibility for a major piece of the business. I'd like to think I'll have experience in many parts of the business over time.*

You don't want to spout off various job titles or a specific position. You never know what kinds of duties and jobs will be obsolete by the time you reach the end of your career, especially in fields that are always changing (such as computer technology). Instead, focus on the experiences you would like to have in your career, and the things you would like to be responsible for. Even though this question does ask about your long-term goals, be sure to stay realistic and keep your goals along the same career path.

Q: **Have you ever taken a position that didn't fit into your long-term plan?**

*How to **answer** it: Though I had always been drawn to a high-tech career, I was offered a very lucrative position in real estate several years back. Though I knew that real estate was not my life work, I decided to take the job for financial security. Before long, I realized that the work wasn't fulfilling or challenging enough to keep me happy. I stayed with the company for two years, but I remained close to many of my original contacts in the high-tech industry, and I was lucky enough to pick up where I'd left off. I've since moved up in the ranks, and my long-term plans include staying in the industry and assuming greater responsibility in the area of computer programming and networking.*

Don't be afraid to answer no to this question. Many members of the work force have been lucky enough to develop a strong and compatible career path right off the bat, and stick to it throughout their careers. If this is the case with you, don't be afraid to tell the interviewer so. If you have taken a job that didn't quite fit in with what you hoped to accomplish, talk about the reasons that led to this acceptance. The interviewer is trying to determine how wisely you can pick jobs to match your interests and aspirations. If you've been sidetracked by some job, you'll probably have to convince the recruiter that you are on the right track pursuing this position.

 Have you progressed in your career as you expected?

> *How to answer it:* My six years with a major gas company have included solid experience in price analysis, capital budgets, and financial planning. I now believe I'm ready to take on departmental responsibility for the entire finance function within a finance company.

Think about your past career experiences. Have you accomplished as much as you had hoped to at this point? If not, why do you think that is? Talk about the many learning experiences you've had and what these have taught you about the industry. Be realistic in admitting the areas where you need more experience. Honesty—without demonstrating either pessimism or unrealistic expectations—is important when answering this question.

Interest in Your Chosen Career

 Why did you choose this career?

> *How to answer it:* When I started college, I wasn't sure what I wanted to do. I visited the career office, and they gave me some self-assessment tests. Based on the results, they gave me a list of careers that might be suitable and told me how to research them. I did, and this is what I thought I'd like best.

Great answer. This is someone who knows what steps to take to make an important decision.

Q: **Since this will be your first job, how do you know you'll like the career path?**

*How to **answer** it: Although it's true that I've never worked in this industry, I've talked to many friends and alums at my school who've been successful here. I always ask them what the job's greatest challenges are and what is most rewarding about the job. From the information I've gained, I'm confident that I'll be able to adapt quickly to your culture and will find the next few years rewarding, based on my goals and values.*

Unless you've done your research and/or are really familiar with the industry, this can be a difficult question to answer. Before going into an interview, be sure you know what kind of job—or even job title—you would be next in line for. By taking the position you are applying for, what would be the next logical step, according to your industry's general career path? If you have had any experience in the field—an internship, for example—make sure to mention that. You should also feel free to discuss the conversations you had with professionals within the industry and how you gained a better understanding of the job and the career path through those people. Point out why you are interested in this career, how you've learned more about the industry, and how you are able to keep current with the industry trends.

Q: **What makes you think that this job is right for you at this point in your career?**

*How to **answer** it: Though I have never had the title of manager, I think that my past experiences up until now could have only led me in this direction. I have spent the past five years working as a corporate trainer for two separate Fortune 500 companies. My job required that I learn the functions and responsibilities of each of the companies' departments well enough that I could teach others how to do the job. More than learning the business basics of just about every department*

in a major corporation—from sales and marketing to account-
ing—I have also learned how to deal with people effectively in
an authoritative position. I still get phone calls from people I
have trained in the past asking me questions and telling me
about their own promotions. I think that if you ask any of these
people, they would agree that I would make a great manager.

In addition to addressing your applicable skills, and the logical progression that brought you to apply for this job, address your desire to work for this company in this position. Showcase the knowledge you have of this company and what the specific job entails. Describe the experiences you want to pursue that build on your current skills and interests. Be as specific as you can, based on what you know about the current or future direction of the position and the department. Demonstrate why this position fits with your personal career goals. Talk about how you can create job growth for yourself.

Q: **If you could start all over again, which direction would you take?**

How to answer it: I've always enjoyed consumer sales as
I've moved up in my career. Looking back, I wish I'd gotten a
bit more experience in market research earlier in my career,
because it's important to understand the types of quantita-
tive models and technical research techniques that a regional
sales manager now needs to know.

The interviewer is trying to figure out if the career path you have chosen to take (including this interview) is ideal for you. Is it this industry alone that you are passionate about, or does your heart lie somewhere else? In answering this question, offer some insight as to why your goals may have changed a bit, given the information you have now. The best way to answer this question is to think of a separate but related task that you enjoy and to talk about how you may have chosen to do something with that. Be honest and insightful, but reassure the interviewer that the only place you want to be is with this company.

 How long do you think you'd continue to grow in this job?

*How to **answer** it: I define job growth as the process of acquiring new skills, new knowledge, and new insight into the industry. That said, as long as I can manage this type of growth, I consider myself successful. I'm a believer in stretching a job by reaching out to learn more about other areas peripheral to my job.*

This is a variation on the question of where you want to be in five years. Again, when answering, be as specific as you can based on all you know about the position. Make sure that any goals or time frames you state are realistic and well thought out. Don't mention a job title you'd want next, or the interviewer will wonder if you're already preoccupied with moving on.

 What career path interests you within the company?

*How to **answer** it: I'd like to work toward becoming a senior project manager within your commercial real estate firm. My background includes several areas within commercial real estate, including working in architectural design, with governmental departments and agencies, with banks in the finance area, and, finally, in sales and leasing. I'd like to pull all this background together in the next few years and eventually have project management responsibility.*

In addition to demonstrating your knowledge of the company, or the typical career path within the industry, the interviewer is interested in how realistic you are. Use the knowledge you have of this industry in general and this company in particular to talk about the path you are interested in following. If you're unfamiliar with the typical career path, it's okay to ask a question such as, "What's the typical career path for someone with my skills?" Focus principally on businesses or divisions of the company that interest you, as well as skills and challenges you hope to master in the next few years.

Q: How does this job compare to the other positions you are pursuing?

How to **answer** *it: Since I've narrowed my job search to only those large securities firms within the finance industry, this job is very close to the other types of positions I am currently interviewing for. The basic skills necessary with all of these firms are similar: strong quantitative and analytical abilities, and the ability to make decisions quickly and good interpersonal skills to react to customer needs.*

While the interviewer may not want to hear all about your most recent interviews with the company's biggest competitors, he does want to be assured that you are settled on a career path. He wants to make sure that you are not picking job titles and/or companies out of a hat. Some consistency or thread of commonality among your other prospects is important here. Your choices must reflect your career aspirations. Talk about the common skills that are clearly needed in all the jobs you're pursuing.

Q: Have you ever found yourself really burned out from a job, and if so, what did you do about it?

How to **answer** *it: Because I know how damaging it can be to begin experiencing those sort of feelings, I don't allow myself to get locked into an unchanging routine. I am the type of person who will continually ask for new assignments and tasks so that I can keep motivated and challenged.*

The interviewer is trying to figure out a few different things here. Are you smart and disciplined enough to avoid burnout? When you are not being productive, do you recognize it? What do you do to cope with stress? The interviewer wants to be sure that in a few months, you will not be running from this job and company.

Focus principally on businesses or divisions of the company that interest you, as well as skills and challenges you hope to master in the next few years.

Personal Interests, Hobbies, and Activities

 Do you have any hobbies?

How to answer it: I love woodworking. I've made tables, chairs, and a bookshelf. I love the satisfaction I get from taking a few pieces of wood and turning them into something I, or someone else, can use.

This answer shows that the interviewee can see a project through from beginning to end.

 Other than work, tell me about an activity you've remained interested in over several years.

How to answer it: I've been involved in fundraising efforts for cancer research ever since my grandmother died from breast cancer. I'm hoping that the research can save the lives of others.

The interviewer is questioning whether you are fickle. Do you take a strong interest in things and stick to them, or do you seem to have a problem with commitment? Prove to the interviewer that you are a solid person who doesn't just jump into something to jump right back out. Talk about your hobbies and favorite activities. Think about the other questions that the interviewer is considering: Are your interests compatible with the job you are applying for? Would they be of value in any way to the company?

Q: What do you do in your spare time?

*How to **answer** it: I am a real sports fan. Whether watching or playing, I enjoy the excitement that sports such as baseball, basketball, and tennis have to offer. I especially enjoy team sports. Knowing that a group of people is working so closely together to achieve a specific goal is inspiring to me in many ways. I know that many of your clients are high-profile sports clubs and companies, and I think that because of my dedication to sports of all kinds, I could definitely bring a unique perspective and insight to the company.*

The interviewer wants evidence that you're well rounded, not one-dimensional. He is looking for shared interests or common ground. Make sure that the personal life you describe is active and fulfilling. Though the interviewer wants to know that you will be dedicated to your job, he does not want to think that this is the only creative outlet you will have. You should always, in some way, relate your answer to the job description.

Q: Tell me about a time when you were in a recreational setting and got an idea that helped in your work.

*How to **answer** it: I was on vacation in Mexico and saw a woman with a homemade seesaw she was using to lift her laundry basket when she needed something out of it. It gave me an idea for a new type of scaffolding that I designed when I got back to work. Now our brick masons have a rotating bench that keeps their materials at waist level, which reduces back fatigue.*

The interviewer wants to know that—even when you're not working—you are able to synthesize information and apply what you see to your profession. You want to be sure that you are portraying yourself as an innovative and creative person. While you want to show you can be competitive in business, talking about a great idea that you saw another business doing and chose to copy won't showcase your own creative thinking. Show that your work is something you are naturally inquisitive about rather than something you have to do. Are you able to think outside of the box to come up with fresh ideas? Be sure to give specific examples.

Q: **How is your personality reflected in the kinds of activities you enjoy?**

How to answer it: I love to cook and entertain. That's the salesman coming out in me. I love sharing experiences with people, and I'm very outgoing.

Talk about the way your natural skills, values, and ethics are reflected in things you do in your spare time. What do your hobbies and passions outside of work say about your personality? Remember, everything we do says something about us as a person. Think about your words so that the image you portray of yourself is always to your advantage.

Q: **What are some of the things you do to relax?**

How to answer it: The main thing that helps me to relax is my family. For me, my weekends are like a vacation. I make the most of all the time I have to spend with my family. When I'm at work, I focus on what is going on in my professional life, but when I am at home, it's all about my family. When I began working at my present job, my husband and I decided to buy a home about twenty miles outside of the city. It was really one of the best things we ever did; now, even the drive home is relaxing.

The interviewer wants to be reassured that you do not spend all of your time—physically or mentally—in the office. Describe at least one part of your life or activity that you engage in that you find to be relaxing. Talking about what you do in your free time is a great way to give the interviewer an insight into who you are as a person.

Q: **Our company believes that employees should give time back to the community. How do you feel about that?**

How to answer it: I completely agree. In my last job as a manager, I allowed employees to spend one day a month, as long as the entire staff wasn't gone on one day, giving back to the community as a volunteer. I myself spend one Friday a month working with an adult literacy program.

If you have spent time giving back to your community in some way, this is a great time to talk about it. Even if you have not, this is a good opportunity for you to discuss the issues, charities, and world problems that concern you. If you were given the time to participate in community outreach, what would you do? Showing a lack of excitement at the prospect of helping others is probably not the type of spirit a company is looking for. Do you use your skills productively? Are you unselfish and a real team player? Demonstrate how your personal interests make you productive even when you aren't being paid. What incentives other than a paycheck inspire you?

Q: **Are there any community projects that have benefited from your professional experience?**

How to answer it: As a marketing professional, I have been able to help out at our local high school in drumming up pub-licity and awareness for its fundraisers.

This question gives the interviewer a sense of your values and lets her know whether you will be a good corporate citizen. Showing that you like to apply your professional expertise to situations in which the only reward is good will impresses an interviewer. Don't get sidetracked describing a cause that doesn't demonstrate job-related skills. Avoid discussing any charity or organization that may be considered controversial; the last thing you want to do is offend the interviewer.

Q: **Describe how a sport or hobby taught you a lesson in teamwork or discipline.**

How to ***answer*** *it: I used to play football, and our coach always taught us that the most important part of the game was watching out for the other guy, that if you do that job well, you'll always have someone watching out for you as well. It is exactly this strategy that I have tried to apply in my professional life. Help out when and where you can, and you'll always have others to rely on as well.*

Remember that the key to this question is teamwork! Rather than focus on how you have applied a certain strategy to work to your advantage, talk about how you have used lessons learned to help your entire department or work group or a time when you had to use teamwork to get a desired result. Tell a specific story, then describe how the same skill or lesson has been used in your work.

Q: **Tell me about an interest that you outgrew.**

How to ***answer*** *it: Early on, I wanted to be a research physician. Then I spent time in a chemistry lab and realized that I wasn't looking forward to the next two years of lab work. That's why I've chosen marketing for medical equipment instead. It combines my respect for the medical profession with a job that's more suited to my personality.*

Describe a former interest or hobby that you no longer pursue, making sure that the interest isn't related in some way to the job you're interviewing for. You also don't want to expose a weak skill that the interviewer had never even considered. Talk about why you outgrew that interest and why it's not compatible with your current interests. Be sure to discuss how your current interests are related to your career.

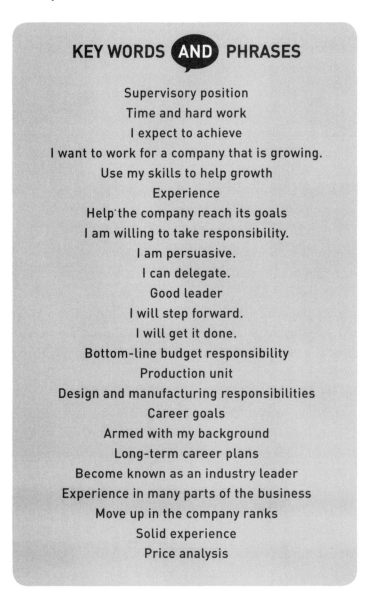

KEY WORDS AND PHRASES

Supervisory position
Time and hard work
I expect to achieve
I want to work for a company that is growing.
Use my skills to help growth
Experience
Help the company reach its goals
I am willing to take responsibility.
I am persuasive.
I can delegate.
Good leader
I will step forward.
I will get it done.
Bottom-line budget responsibility
Production unit
Design and manufacturing responsibilities
Career goals
Armed with my background
Long-term career plans
Become known as an industry leader
Experience in many parts of the business
Move up in the company ranks
Solid experience
Price analysis

Capital budgets
Financial planning
Self-assessment
What is most rewarding
Adapt quickly to the company culture
Functions and responsibilities
Authoritative position
Market research information
Quantitative models
Technical research techniques
Insight into the industry
Stretch a job by reaching out
Senior project manager
Background
Basic skills necessary
Quantitative and analytical abilities
Can make decisions quickly
Good interpersonal skills
Motivated
Challenged
Fundraising skills
Specific goals
Unique perspective and insight
Synthesize information
Creative thinking
Sharing experiences with other people
Give back to the community
Incentives
Values
A job suited to my personality

Chapter 5

Showcasing
Why You're a
Good Fit

YOU CAN ELIMINATE YOURSELF FROM THE RUNNING FOR ANY JOB IF YOU DON'T research the position properly. You need to determine whether you will be able to thrive in a particular job with a particular employer, and you need to convince your interviewer that your compatibility will benefit the company. Interviewers use many different questions to gauge your compatibility with a particular company and position, and this chapter focuses on preparing you to answer them well.

Business Sense and Personal Character

Q: **Give an example of how you saw a project through, despite various obstacles.**

*How to **answer** it: My promotion from account representative to account manager required that I pass on many of my oldest accounts to the new account representative. After two years of dealing directly with me, some of these accounts did not take kindly to a new face. Some even threatened to move their accounts if I could not be part of their projects. While I had plenty of work to do adjusting to my new job, I assigned* *myself the role of account advisor to all of the accounts who were having problems adjusting. I took the time to visit each of these accounts personally with the new account rep and discuss the changes that were taking place within our company. I assured each of the accounts that I would be there for them if they needed answers, but that they should refer to the new rep with any new business. After a few months of phone calls, they eventually began to stop. The accounts realized that my replacement had a lot of talent, and they began to trust in his abilities. To this day, each of those accounts is still with my company.*

The goal in your answer is to demonstrate your competence and willingness to do well, even when the pressure's on. Don't dwell on the obstacles themselves; the interviewer doesn't care about the problems of your current or former company. Focus your answer on how you approached these obstacles and the results that you got.

Q: **Tell me about a time when you showed real determination.**

*How to **answer** it: A few years back, our workforce was predominantly older baby boomers who were not web savvy. When my company went online, nobody seemed to appreciate what the technology could do for our business. Most of the employees weren't sure what to do. I was convinced that if all staff members took the time to learn for online training, they would all find it a much easier way to do business. I began a promotion in which each morning I would send out via e-mail a trivia contest. The first person to get all answers right and send them back via e-mail would win a prize. As the employees became more comfortable using e-mail to enter the trivia contest, they began using the Internet to help them conduct business as well.*

Talk about a time when you persevered to accomplish a goal. You can use either a professional or a personal goal here, as long as it reflects an interest in developing new skills. Demonstrate your ability to gather resources, predict obstacles, and manage stress. Talk about the results you obtained.

 Tell me about a time when you showed real diligence or perseverance.

*How to **answer** it:* I was working on an installation project when about halfway through to completion, the client decided that he wanted something different. While for many this would cause quite an obstacle, my partner and I agreed that we could still get the work done by the original completion date. We had to put in about seventy hours a week for the next few months, but we did it to make sure that the client was happy and the project went according to plan.

Talk about your professional character. Describe your focus, diligence, and accountability. Demonstrate how you gather resources, manage your time wisely, or are willing to go the extra mile. Use a specific example from your professional, educational, or personal history. Don't paint a somewhat problematic picture of yourself. There's a big difference between being determined and just plain annoying and tiring.

 How many days were you absent from work in the past year, and why?

*How to **answer** it:* I was absent from work three days last year. I caught the flu early in the year and was forced to miss two days, and I experienced a death in the family just last month and took a day off.

A history of absenteeism, tardiness, or any indication of a weak work ethic can be detrimental to your candidacy. Answering this question should be an easy way to score points. If you used up all of your sick and/or personal days, tell the interviewer the reason. Be honest; lying will be found out. If you think your poor attendance may be a source of bad references, be prepared to give a detailed and exonerating explanation of why you have missed so much work in the past. Most importantly, convince the interviewer of your dependability and assure her that punctuality and/or absenteeism is not something she should worry about.

Q: Are you punctual?

*How to **answer** it: Yes. In the past year, I have only been late to work on one or two occasions, and each time I called my supervisor ahead of time to let him know. On each occasion, it was a matter of traffic delays.*

This is really just an alternate version of the previous question. The problem here is that whereas there is a definitive answer to the earlier question ("I was out three days."), this question is much more open-ended. Again, to say yes to this question when you know that you are always tardy will certainly come back to haunt you.

Q: We have found that all of our employees fall into one of two categories: concept oriented or task oriented. Which of these categories do you fit into?

*How to **answer** it: When given a project, I like to be involved in every step. From initial development to final product, I like to be able to use my creativity and strong problem-solving abilities. I would definitely consider myself more concept oriented.*

Don't slight the question by coming up with an all-encompassing answer ("I've got a little bit of both in me!"). Choose a side and stay there. Describe some of your personal characteristics that made you choose this orientation. Most importantly, be sure that the answer you choose coincides with the job description. If you are to be engaged in manual labor forty hours a week, it is not likely that your orientation toward concepts will help you in any way. Similarly, if your job entails a lot of creativity, being task oriented is not necessarily the best way to be. Whatever answer you come up with, relate it to the job in some way.

Q: **What would your supervisor tell me about your attention to detail?**

> *How to **answer** it: As my supervisor relies heavily on me to think projects through with him, I am confident that he would praise my attention to detail. I know how easy it can be for someone to overlook the smallest details of a project, and I pride myself on catching any glitches before they find their way into the final results.*

Regardless of the job you hold or the industry you belong to, a strong attention to detail is a great asset. Throughout the day, there are so many small details that often get overlooked that it is comforting for employers to know they have employees they can count on. If your attention to detail track record is not the best, don't try and push off the importance of this trait by discussing another one of your strengths. Instead, admit that you have let mistakes get past you before, but talk about how you are working to stop this. If you do, in fact, have a strong attention to detail, talk about an experience when this really helped you in some way.

Q: **Describe a professional skill you've been able to acquire in your current position or at your current company.**

> *How to **answer** it: While I had used computers quite extensively in my previous positions, I had never been required to use database technology. As my current company relies heavily upon several different databases to store all of our work,*

I have become an expert in programs such as Access. What used to take me hours of research and data compiling can now be completed with just a few clicks of the mouse.

The best way to answer this question is to talk about a new skill that you have learned—and worked toward mastering—while at your current job. Though it is okay to talk about a skill that you have been able to improve upon in your current job, you don't want to raise any unnecessary red flags. You certainly don't want to draw attention to negative aspects of your professional abilities, even if they're in the past and it's something you've worked toward overcoming. You want to make sure that the interviewer sees you as a desirable candidate who is able and ready to take on new tasks with enthusiasm.

Q: Why is service such an important issue?

*How to **answer** it: Asking why service is important would be the same as asking why customers are important; it is the heart and soul of any business. You can't have a business without customers, and you can't maintain customers without a strong dedication to service. If a customer isn't receiving a level of service that meets or exceeds his expectations, you can be sure he will take his business elsewhere. And it's likely that he will relay that information to other would-be customers. On the other hand, if you are dedicated to providing the best service you can, customers will keep coming back for more, and they'll still tell others about you. In many instances, service may be the one thing that distinguishes a company from the competition. A bad reputation for service may compromise a company's position in the marketplace.*

A question like this gauges your business sense. The interviewer is trying to determine whether you understand the importance of good customer service in establishing a positive image in the marketplace. If possible, talk about how you or your company have taken steps to ensure good customer service and how that has proven beneficial. Show that you understand the impact of repeat business, and convince the interviewer that you will work hard to uphold a standard of good service.

Q: Tell me about a time when you had to deal with an angry customer. How did you handle the situation?

*How to **answer** it: As you can imagine, in the retail world, you are forced to deal with irate customers from time to time, regardless of how strong your product or customer service is. I specifically remember one occasion in which a customer was angry because the item she had purchased was not working properly once she got it home. The best way to handle these situations, in my opinion, is to remember that there is a simple solution. Products can be fixed, exchanged, or refunded. I try to think of myself in terms of the consumer. When discussing the problem with the customer, I speak in a calm, even voice, thus prompting the customer to do the same. The main issue to be concerned with is solving the problem at hand, and you need to be professional enough to get that done.*

How you react to an unsatisfied customer is very important in most positions, and it's especially important if you work in a service industry. The interviewer will be looking for evidence of your aptitude for work that involves a great deal of contact with the public, even in situations in which the public isn't being too nice. Give an example of a time when you were faced with a difficult person and how you handled it. Explain the result of that situation, if in fact something positive came out of it (for example, if the customer reordered a week later). Your answer should illustrate your maturity, diplomacy, and awareness of the needs and feelings of others. Though you shouldn't take such things personally, you should be able to show compassion to the customers who are in need of pacification.

Q: **Are there any issues in your personal life that might in some way affect your professional career?**

*How to **answer** it: I really pride myself on my keen ability to separate my personal life from my work life. When I'm in the office, I am an employee of the company. I recognize this is not the place for me to deal with or worry about issues in my personal life. I do my best to keep a strong work-life balance that keeps both components satisfied.*

The interviewer wants to make sure that you're not going to be bringing your home life to work with you. If you are dealing with stressful personal issues, the company wants to be sure that your time spent at work will be concentrated on work only. Though certain questions about your beliefs or your family are illegal, the interviewer wants to know whether you will be able to perform the duties this job calls for. In the health services industry, for example, personal issues that have not been worked through properly could easily affect your judgment in assessing patients, planning treatments, and making recommendations. Make sure the interviewer knows that you are a fully integrated individual and that your professional life and personal life always remain separate. Today, most employers respect childcare and eldercare issues, but calling attention to them in the interview is an unnecessary red flag.

Q: **Tell me about a time when your diplomacy skills were really put to the test.**

*How to **answer** it: I recall one time when a customer came into the store and demanded his money back on a suit that had apparently been worn. Because this kind of situation happens often—people want a fancy outfit to wear for one night only—*

we have a strict policy that says there are no refunds once the tags have been removed. The man claimed that the suit had become very worn looking after being sent to the dry cleaner and that the cleaner had claimed it was a faulty fabric. Rather than argue with the man about the policy and about the fact that the tags had been removed, I refunded his money, though I didn't believe that he was being honest. He was a consistent customer, and I decided it was more important to maintain his regular business and to keep the other customers from hearing him complain rather than have them doubt the quality of our merchandise.

Diplomacy involves using tact, finesse, and good judgment to reach an end that is ultimately beneficial to the entire company. Being diplomatic for selfish reasons is closer to backhandedness. In answering this question, make sure you demonstrate a pragmatic sensibility. Talk about a problem situation with a client or a work associate that you resolved by remaining objective. How did you show empathy and build rapport? What was the end result? How did this help all those involved, including yourself?

Q: What personal skill or work habit have you struggled to improve?

*How to **answer** it: I think that one habit I have worked very hard to overcome is my inability to say no. I used to be helpful to the point of overextension. It didn't matter that I already had a full plate or whether or not I thought I could do a good job on a project; I would simply always say yes when colleagues asked me for help. Now, when someone asks me to do something for her, I counter with something I'd like help with in return. Since then, cooperation in my office has improved considerably.*

Here's another one of those questions that forces you to confront a negative aspect of your professional character. The interviewer wants to hear about a particular skill that you have had trouble acquiring, or something about yourself that you have had to change for the betterment of the workplace. The smartest way to answer this question is to find an example from your earliest days in the workplace so that any sort of negative quality can be attributed to your lack of experience. Talking about a problem that you have been trying to overcome in your current job will only show the interviewer that that trait could follow you to your new place of business. In the end, make sure you leave no question in the interviewer's mind as to whether that particular work habit is still an obstacle.

Why You Want the Job

Q: **After learning more about this job, which aspect interests you most?**

How to **answer** *it: I'm particularly interested in your recent joint ventures with two processing companies in Latin America. My father was an army officer, so we lived in Latin America for three years. I am very interested in seeing what happens with these agreements. What are your plans for the next few years?*

In the section regarding your motivation, the interviewer asks a very similar question: What particular aspect of the company interests you most? Essentially, there is no real difference between these questions except the way that they are worded. In the question above, you are being asked to talk directly about the company in an effort to prove that you have done your research. In this instance, you should feel free to talk about the company or about the position itself. Describe your qualifications for the job and how well the job fits your natural skills and abilities.

Give evidence that you've performed well in similar work. What proof can you offer that you'll excel in this job? The best answer to this question would address both the company and the position. More specifically, it would focus on what you could do for the company in the position at hand. If you've researched the company properly, you should have no problem answering this question quickly and authoritatively.

Q: After learning more about this job, which aspect interests you least?

How to answer it: In my last position, I was able to find more success by spending time on my major accounts rather than scheduling one-on-one interviews with smaller accounts. Though every salesperson has her preference, I think that this is really where my strength lies. In my time there, I was able to increase my key account business by 20 percent. I would like to be able to continue with this personal style within your company to obtain even better results.

This is another one of those questions that job seekers hate to be asked. Forcing you to talk about a potentially negative aspect of the job can be a little intimidating, especially when you're trying to impress this person. One way to skirt the issue is to talk about a situation in your current position that you find to be a negative aspect and find out whether this job would have a similar downside. Another way to counter this question is to ask why the last person left the job. Respond to the interviewer's answer, then go on to discuss what you see as the positive points of this job, even if you've done so before.

Q: What aspects of this job do you feel most confident about?

How to answer it: As the companies I have worked with in the past have been engaged in the manufacture of very similar products, I feel that I will be able to fully integrate myself in no time at all. With a strong knowledge of your company's products, I think I will be able to jump right in with lots of creative and fresh ideas and translate my past success to your company.

Make sure that when you answer this question, you sell the skills you have as they relate to this job—and not just sell yourself! The interviewer probably already has a good sense of your personality and you as a person; this is a chance to plug your applicable skills and how they relate to the position at hand. Talk about your skills in relation to the larger scope of things: that is, how they relate to this job, this company, and the industry.

 What concerns you most about performing this job?

*How to **answer** it: As my past experiences relate directly to this position, I am confident that I could perform the job well. Other than that, I have never been the key manager of a department, and I am a little concerned as to whether or not there will be a large enough customer service network. As one of the key points of this company is a twenty-four-hour service line, I just want to be sure that there are always enough people here to answer the phones.*

Even if the job you are interviewing for will bring about many brand-new responsibilities and is not something you have much experience with, you should never say the word "failure." Always project an air of confidence. One way you can answer this question is to turn it around and say, "Nothing that you have mentioned so far concerns me. I am fairly confident that I could perform the job really well. Are there any aspects of this job that you are concerned with me performing?" If the interviewer comes back with a few questions, respond with the same confidence in your abilities. Address each one of the recruiter's concerns and make her sure that your interests are compatible with the position. Offer proof that will dispel any doubts she may have.

Q: **Why is this a particularly good job for someone with your qualifications?**

*How to **answer** it:* Based on what you've told me about the last person who held—and excelled in—this job, I believe we share many similarities and, therefore, am confident that I would do a great job. We seem to have the same educational qualifications and similar work experience. I also think that I would work well with your audit team. I come from a similar kind of environment and know exactly what a client can do to make the consulting relationship more productive.

The key to answering this question is to draw upon experiences from your current or former job and talk about the positive experiences you have had. If you know anything about the success and background of the person who formerly held this position, that's also a great way to prove that you are a great match for the job. Being too specific can be detrimental to this question, as it indicates that you may not quite understand what this position is all about.

What You'd Bring to the Company

Q: **The department you would be in charge of hasn't had a supervisor in months. This is going to be a big transition for the staff. How will you handle it?**

*How to **answer** it:* I wouldn't want to make any big changes for at least the first two weeks. I find it's better to just observe how things are done before trying to make any improvements. I want to gain the staff's trust first and listen to their concerns.

This candidate has a plan in place, and she lays it out step by step. She knows that employees who have been unsupervised for a long time need to get used to having someone overseeing their work.

 Senior citizens represent a huge market now, and we want to convince them to buy our product. If we hired you, how would you help with that?

*How to **answer** it: In addition to being a very big market, the senior market also continues to grow. They are a group with a very active lifestyle. Many have expendable income, and they choose to use their savings on travel, so it's clear we have a product they will want. We have to determine how to reach them. I would first want to do research to find out what publications seniors read and what television shows they watch. Only then can we embark on an advertising campaign.*

This candidate demonstrates that he would take a methodical approach to this project. He also shows that he understands the market very well.

Q: **We're about to change over to a new software program for our shipping and receiving department. We'd like the person we hire for this position to do the training. Are you the right person for that job?**

*How to **answer** it: I am definitely the right person for this job. As you can see on my resume, my last job was with a software distributor. One of my responsibilities was to travel to our clients' offices to provide software training.*

This is one confident candidate.

Q: **The person who last held this position took ill and has only been able to work off and on for the last three months and has finally resigned. Things are a huge**

mess, which the person we hire will need to sort out. Are you up for the challenge?

*How to **answer** it: I love a good challenge. First I'll sort through the mess to organize it. Then I'll see which things require immediate attention and which things I can work on later.*

The interviewee, by giving this answer, shows that she knows how to both organize and prioritize. These are two skills that are extremely important for someone taking over a job that has been neglected.

Q: The person we hire will have to respond to customer complaints occasionally. Will you be able to do that?

*How to **answer** it: Years ago I worked in customer service. I'll be able to put that experience to good use.*

The interviewee finds some past experience that will help her with this aspect of the job.

Q: In about a year, we want to open a new branch on the other side of town. We plan to train the person who takes this position to run that office. Is that something you'd be interested in?

*How to **answer** it: I would welcome that opportunity if it arises.*

Notice the applicant says, "If it arises." She wants to express her eagerness to take on more responsibility with this employer without sounding like she'd leave if that opportunity didn't come up, or if such an opportunity came up sooner with another company.

Q: If we hire you, will you be willing to get your certification? You have all the skills we're looking for, but we really need someone who is certified.

How to **answer** *it: I was planning to take my certification exam in June. That's the next time it's being given.*

While it would have been okay for this candidate to say he would get his certification because the client has asked him to, it's even better that he said he was planning to do it anyway.

Q: We have several clients with outstanding bills. If we hire you, how will you handle this situation?

How to **answer** *it: First, I would want to go through the paperwork to make sure these clients were properly notified their accounts are delinquent. If I find out they were notified, I'll call each one personally to discuss this. There might be extenuating circumstances. It's important not to be too heavy-handed in dealing with these types of situations. After all, these are our clients. We don't want to lose them entirely.*

This candidate gives a clearly thought-out answer. She knows how important it is to be diplomatic when dealing with clients.

Q: Our clients expect a very quick turnaround on the projects we do for them. Can you handle that?

How to **answer** *it: Yes, I can. While I was in graduate school, I had several professors who assigned projects that were due only a few days later. I became an expert at scheduling my time around completing these assignments.*

Since this interviewee doesn't have work experience to draw upon, she talks about her experience as a student. In the process she highlights a valuable skill—time management.

Q: **If you are hired for this position, you will go from managing your current staff of ten to managing fifty people. Will you be able to oversee a substantially larger staff?**

How to answer it: Yes, I will. Although I've never managed a staff of that size before, I know I have the skills necessary to do it. I am a strong leader. I am good at communicating what each member of my staff needs to accomplish. I am good at delegating responsibilities, which will be even more important with such a large staff.

This candidate lets the interviewer know that he has all the skills that a good manager should have, even though he doesn't have experience with the exact situation he will face.

Q: **When we are in the process of developing a new product, it's essential that information about it doesn't leak out. How are you at keeping secrets?**

How to answer it: After working in the technology field for the past three years, I know how important it is to keep information confidential until a product is released.

This candidate knows from experience that keeping secrets is important.

Q: **We currently have several employees who have problems with things like tardiness and excessive personal phone calls. How would you deal with this if we hired you as supervisor?**

How to answer it: First, I would need to find out exactly what is occurring. Then, prior to singling out any one employee, I would circulate a memo to the entire department that reiterated the rules. If the behavior continued, I would have a private meeting with each employee who isn't following the rules. I would stress the importance of following the rule they are *breaking, and I would try to find out if there are extenuating circumstances that could be remedied. If the employee continues to break the rules, there would be repercussions.*

This interviewee is clearly not one to "leap without looking." She knows how important it is to evaluate a situation before taking action. However, she will take action in an expedient manner.

Q: **Four times a year we work around the clock for about a week. Will that be a problem?**

*How to **answer** it: That's fine with me. I understand that the beginning of each season is a very busy time.*

Not only is this job candidate willing to work late, he knows enough about the industry to know what times of year this would be expected of him.

Q: **Would I be able to trust you, as my assistant, to take over for me whenever I'm out of the office?**

*How to **answer** it: Absolutely. I would follow whatever rules you set forth. I also have excellent judgment, so I can handle whatever comes up.*

The applicant uses this opportunity to highlight her skills.

Q: **Whoever fills this position will need to write next year's budget, which needs to be 10 percent lower than the current one. Could you do this?**

*How to **answer** it: I had to do something similar when my department went through funding cuts last year and I was in charge of writing the new budget. First I reviewed the current year's budget and removed amounts that had been budgeted for one-time events. I found a few areas where our actual expenditures were lower than we had budgeted, and I was able to bring*

the amount down to more realistic levels, of course account-
ing for possible price increases. Finally, I went through it to
see what cuts would have a minimal effect on services. I cut a
program that had very low attendance. This eliminated the need
to hire a part-time instructor. I was able to submit a budget that
was 12 percent lower than the one for the previous year.

This candidate demonstrates how he takes a practical approach
to trimming a budget. He shows how he is able to get the job done
with a minimal effect on service.

Q: **As a contact person for our clients, you might have
to tell them little white lies to keep them happy. For
example, we never would want a client to know about a
mishap that occurred with a project we were working on
for them. Would you be comfortable with that?**

*How to **answer** it: I'm always inclined to be honest. However,
I know that little white lies come with the territory in this field.
If not telling a client the whole truth keeps them calm and
happy, then I can do that. No need to worry anyone unnec-
essarily. Of course, I will work to make sure the problem is
resolved as quickly as possible.*

Knowing what common practice is in her field helps this candidate
answer this question. By telling the interviewer that she always
tries to be honest but is willing to tell a client a white lie to keep
him happy, she essentially says to the interviewer, "I'll always be
honest with you, but I'll also help protect your relationship with
clients even if it means telling the occasional half-truth."

Q: **The students in this school can be very challenging to
manage. As a teacher here, will you be able to handle
them?**

*How to **answer** it:* *I worked with special-needs children when I was an assistant teacher at Ardsley School. I learned that it is important to look at each child as an individual. Each one has different strengths and weaknesses. If you look at it that way, you can figure out what strategy you need to use to work with each child. Children will trust you when they know you see them as individuals and will usually respond by doing what you need them to do.*

Although this candidate is applying for his first professional job, he is able to draw on his past experience. He explains what he learned from his previous experience as an assistant teacher.

 In this fast-paced environment, we need someone who can think on her feet. Are you that person?

*How to **answer** it:* *Yes, I am. I have experience making thoughtful decisions under pressure. I worked at a daily newspaper for five years. Every day we had to make last-minute decisions about what to include in the next day's edition. There was no time to waste when the paper had to go to press within the next half-hour.*

This candidate shows how her experience has enabled her to be decisive.

Your Past Work Experiences

 What was your first job?

*How to **answer** it:* *My very first job was in a deli. I worked there every summer from ninth grade until I graduated from college. At first I was hired to do odd jobs, but once I was old enough, I worked behind the counter, serving customers. I was*

the youngest employee there, but my boss always said I was the hardest-working one.

Although this job was unrelated to his career, his longevity there, as well as his former boss's opinion of him, lets the interviewer know that he was a valuable employee.

 Out of the jobs you've had, which was your favorite?

*How to **answer** it: My favorite job was teaching at the Wee Ones Preschool. I like my current job at Parkside Elementary, but I realize now that I prefer to work with preschoolers. That's why I want to work here.*

This candidate has chosen a job that is related to the one that she is being interviewed for.

 What kinds of jobs did you have during college?

*How to **answer** it: I had a variety of jobs while I was going to college, and since I was paying my own way, I sometimes had more than one job. I worked as a waiter, a door-to-door sales-man, and a data entry clerk. I learned a lot about interacting tactfully with different people, and I also developed my office and computer skills.*

In addition to demonstrating how industrious he is (working his way through school), this candidate shows how he developed skills in different areas through his experience.

 I see three jobs listed on your resume. Can you tell me what you learned from each of them?

*How to **answer** it: I learned a lot on each of my jobs, so it's hard to pick one thing from each, but I'll try. When I worked in customer support at CSV, I learned how to help our*

software users troubleshoot problems. When I worked as a software trainer at Circle Tech, I learned that I needed to find a common ground when teaching a large group of people, because not everyone has the same level of skills. I learned to manage employees at my job as assistant to the head of training at APCO.

Knowing about the job that he's applying for helped the applicant answer this question. He has picked one skill from each job that will be required for the job with this employer.

 Do you find your job rewarding?

*How to **answer** it: I found my job very rewarding for a long time. It hasn't been as rewarding lately. While I love my new responsibilities, I miss working with clients. That is what attracted me to this position—the combination of supervisory responsibilities and client contact.*

It's okay for the interviewee to say she doesn't find her current job rewarding. She explains why she feels this way without placing blame anywhere. With this answer, she also shows that she knows about the position she's interviewing for and explains why she is better suited for it.

 What about your current job isn't very rewarding?

*How to **answer** it: I think every job has something about it that isn't rewarding. There is a lot of paperwork, and I don't find that particularly rewarding, but I know it needs to be done.*

This candidate understands the reality of work. Some job duties are rewarding, while others are not. She chose something that many people don't find particularly rewarding—paperwork.

How have your other jobs prepared you for the one at this company?

How to ***answer*** *it: I've worked on the retail end of the office supplies industry for the past ten years. I know what customers want and in turn what the retail outlets want. I know the industry, and I know the products. That is what qualifies me to be a sales rep for Roxy Staple Company.*

This candidate is confident of his abilities and that comes across in his response.

 Have you had to do any traveling for work?

How to ***answer*** *it: I've had to do some traveling for my job. I went to Asia several times. I enjoy traveling and hope to do more of it on this job. I find it helpful to have face-to-face meetings with clients periodically rather than doing everything through conference calls.*

This applicant knows that his potential employer requires extensive traveling, and although he hasn't done a lot of it, he makes sure to point out that it's something he wants to do more of.

 You've never worked in widget manufacturing before. How have your jobs in the publishing industry prepared you for this?

How to ***answer*** *it: Taking a product, whether it's a widget or a book, from its inception to the hands of the consumer takes a lot of planning. You have to put together a budget and set deadlines. You need to make sure your current staff can handle the work and hire consultants if necessary. You may even have to handle crises along the way, should problems arise. I dealt with such things on a daily basis while working in publishing, and I would be able to use the same planning and management skills to help your company.*

By focusing on his job responsibilities and talking about them in general terms, this candidate is able to show how he can transfer his skills from one industry to another.

Q: **What decisions have you had to make in your current job?**

*How to **answer** it: When I planned career workshops for students, I had to decide what topics to feature, when to hold the workshops, and who would speak at them. I had to decide what software to purchase for our public computers, within the constraints of our budget. I also made decisions about hiring and firing student aides.*

By giving specific examples, this candidate highlights her skills in planning events, making purchasing decisions, working within a budget, and making personnel decisions.

Q: **How is your present job different from the ones you had before it?**

*How to **answer** it: As a senior accounting clerk, I supervise three payroll clerks and a bookkeeper. This is the first time I've had to supervise other people.*

This applicant talks about how she has increased responsibilities at her job.

Q: **What duties of your last job did you find difficult?**

*How to **answer** it: I found it difficult to fire people. Even though I always put a lot of thought into deciding whether or not to terminate someone, I knew I was affecting someone's livelihood.*

No one could fault someone for disliking this unpleasant duty.

Q: **What do you think this job offers that your last job did not?**

*How to **answer** it:* *This job offers me the opportunity to use my research skills. I have mostly administrative duties in my current job, with some research duties. I look forward to a job that is primarily research-oriented with some administrative duties.*

This applicant has both administrative and research skills, as she points out to the interviewer. She wants to use them in a different way than she does in her current job.

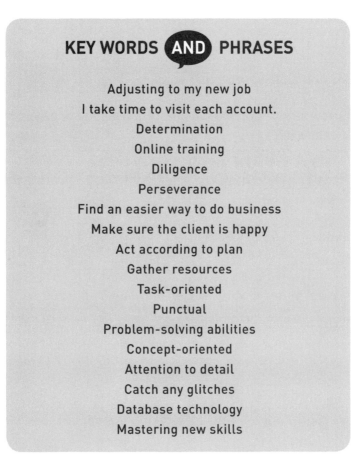

KEY WORDS **AND** PHRASES

Adjusting to my new job
I take time to visit each account.
Determination
Online training
Diligence
Perseverance
Find an easier way to do business
Make sure the client is happy
Act according to plan
Gather resources
Task-oriented
Punctual
Problem-solving abilities
Concept-oriented
Attention to detail
Catch any glitches
Database technology
Mastering new skills

The heart and soul of the business
Strong dedication to service
Service can distinguish us from competition
Calm, even voice
Solve the problem at hand
Separate work life from personal life
Strong work-life balance
Tact
Finesse
Good judgment
Helpful
Cooperation
Motivation
My qualifications for the job
My natural skills and abilities
Spending time on my major accounts
Personal style
Obtain better results
I will be able to fully integrate myself.
Strong knowledge of the company's products
Translate my past success to your company
I could perform the job well.
Key manager of a department
Customer service network
Air of confidence
Educational qualifications
Similar work experience
Make relationships productive
Observe how things are done
Gain my staff's trust
I'm the right person for this job.
Things that require immediate attention
Put my experience to good use

Welcome new opportunities
Certification exam
Expert at scheduling my time
I am good at communicating to my staff.
Confidential information
I will follow the rules.
Excellent judgment
Practical approach
Honest
Thoughtful decisions under pressure
Hard working
I've had a variety of jobs.
Interact tactfully with others
I learn from each of my jobs.
Rewarding
What attracts me to this position
What retail customers want
Planning
Setting deadlines
Decisions about hiring and firing

Chapter 6

Highlighting Your **Ambition** and **Knowledge**

YOUR INTERVIEWER WILL ASK YOU SPECIFIC QUESTIONS TO GAUGE YOUR ENTHUSIASM for the job and your motivation to do it well. You can leave a positive impression if you tailor your answers to highlight your interest in the industry and the company. This is a prime place to showcase the research you've done without being too obvious.

Aside from basic skills, you must show that you are enthusiastic—not just about the prospect of employment but about the industry in general and the company in particular. Find out all you can about a company before you attend the interview. A job candidate who walks into an interview armed with knowledge about the employer demonstrates several things to the interviewer. He demonstrates that he isn't just looking for a job with any employer. He wants to work for this particular company because of what he knows about it. He also shows that he was ambitious enough to do the necessary research to learn what he could about the employer.

The interviewer may test your knowledge about the company by asking you what you can contribute and what changes you would make if you were hired. He may ask you why you want to work for the company and how it fits into your career plans. Using your research, base your answers to these questions upon what you know about the company. It sounds like a cinch, but this chapter will tell you about the potential pitfalls to avoid.

Why You Chose This Industry

 What led you to apply for a position in this industry?

How to **answer** *it: I've always wanted to work in an industry that makes tools. I enjoy working on home improvement projects, so I've collected a number of saws manufactured by your company. I could be an accountant anywhere, but I'd rather work for a company whose products I trust.*

Talk about how you first became interested in this specific industry. Discuss the similarities between your current job and the job you are applying for. Be sure to emphasize that you are looking for a career, not just a job! Make sure that your enthusiasm for the industry—and work in general—comes through in all of your answers (where appropriate, of course).

 Why is it that you have decided to make this industry your career?

How to **answer** *it: The technology in the industry is changing so rapidly that I see lots of room for job enhancement regardless of promotions. I'm particularly interested in the many applications for multimedia as a training tool.*

The interviewer wants to make sure that any time and energy spent on training you will be money well spent and that you will remain with the organization for several years to come. Think about why you have chosen this specific industry or job as a career and what it has to offer you in the future. Don't mention money! You want to assure the interviewer that by selecting you for the job, she is selecting a competent and loyal employee who will look forward to many years of continued growth with the company.

Other key factors to keep in mind when answering this question are what expectations you have for the industry as a whole and what aspects of the business excite you. Though it may seem redundant, the key to a successful interview is to drill your "themes" into the interviewer's head. If you need to mention on more than one occasion your deep interest in the industry or your membership in a professional society, so be it. Be sure to offer specific proof of your long-held interest in the industry and not just your very recent decision to make it your life's career. Passion for your work is one thing that should never be taken for granted.

Q: **Is there anything you find troubling about this industry?**

How to answer it: Actually, no. I've been reading a lot about this industry and everything I've seen so far is positive. This industry has made a great recovery after the decline about a decade ago. Since then it has been growing steadily and actually saw record growth last year.

Although this candidate doesn't have anything negative to say, she takes this opportunity to show that she did her homework.

Q: **Since all your experience has been in another industry, you must be a little concerned about making this change. What do you think working in this industry will be like?**

How to answer it: Everything in this industry seems to go at a very fast pace. I think the transition will be an easy one for me because in the magazine industry, I also worked at a fast pace. There were tight deadlines and sudden changes that needed to be dealt with on a moment's notice. From what I can tell, this industry involves the same things. I think I will be able to make a seamless transition to this industry.

This candidate's answer conveys that he feels he can adapt to working in this new industry.

What You Know about the Company

Q: Tell me what you know about this company.

*How to **answer** it: I served as an intern to a restaurant analyst last summer, so I followed all the steakhouse chains closely. What you've done especially well is focus on a limited menu with great consistency among locations; the business traveler trusts your product everywhere in the United States. I'm particularly interested in your real estate finance group and expansion plans.*

This is one of those open-ended questions that many interviewees hate. It ranks right up there with "Tell me about yourself." Still, if you have done your homework—like you should have—you should have no problem scoring points with this inquiry. Start out by telling the recruiter how you first became aware of the company. Talk about the personal experiences you've had with the company's product or service—whether it be your own experience or someone else's.

Discuss the reasons why a job with this particular company (and not a competitor) would be ideal. What is this company offering that its competitors are not? While a general knowledge of the company is imperative, avoid reciting the company's mission statement. The recruiter is looking for evidence of a genuine interest in the company (not just a general interest in the industry). Make sure you provide him with the insightful information he is looking for.

Q: What particular aspect of the company interests you most?

*How to **answer** it: I'm particularly interested in your recent joint ventures with two processing companies in Latin America.*

When my father was an army officer, we lived in Latin America for three years. I am very interested in what happens with these agreements. What are your plans for the next few years?

This is a great way to showcase your special knowledge of the company. If the company has a website, try to gain access to any recent press releases to learn about the latest happenings. If you've researched the company properly, you should have no problem answering this question quickly and authoritatively.

Q: What do you think it takes to be successful here?

*How to **answer** it: I understand that Q & H Corporation introduced five new products to the market in the last year alone. To be a successful employee of such an innovative company, one would have to be very creative. In a competitive industry such as soaps and toiletries, you need employees who can keep up with what consumers want.*

This person has obviously done her homework. She not only knows about the company, but she seems to know about the industry as well.

Q: How much do you know about our company's recent growth?

*How to **answer** it: I know that XYZ Brands is a multinational company. I was particularly intrigued by your acquisition of ABC Corporation last March. It seems like it's going to open up a whole new market for this company.*

Not only does the interviewee show that she took the time to learn about the company, she also shows she's kept up with the latest news about it. Notice that the interviewee said "it's going to open up a whole new market for this company" not "your company," so as not to create distance between herself and the employer.

What do you know about some of our major clients?

*How to **answer** it: I know your major clients are all in the canned food industry. BBR represents Heller Foods, Green Products, and Acorn Corp. I read in Advertising Digest just last week that Heans hired you to run their new broadcast campaign.*

This candidate has done his homework, even keeping up with the latest industry news.

 What interests you about our products and services?

*How to **answer** it: Turning Corporation provides products and services that help so many people. Just the other day, I was reading about the new motorized scooter Turning developed. Those in health care and advocates for the disabled are very excited about it, according to everything I've read.*

This candidate has obviously made a point of learning about her prospective employer, including keeping up with news about the latest products.

 What is your favorite product made by our company?

*How to **answer** it: I have been using your model X cellular phone for more than two years now. Although friends and colleagues are constantly having problems with cell phones from other manufacturers, I have never experienced any sort of problems. In fact, whenever I head out to buy a new electronic product, I look for your label; I know that it is synonymous with "quality."*

Whether the company you're applying to is product or service based, describe your related personal experiences. If you are interviewing with a restaurant, talk about your favorite thing on the menu. Think about why you use the company's product/service.

If possible, discuss the various other markets that you think the company's product could succeed in. Employers love to hear new ideas from fresh voices.

 If you had the opportunity to develop a new product to add to our line, what would it be?

*How to **answer** it: Since Perfect Posies currently sells flowers and other gift items, I think a line of chocolate would be a good choice. I recently saw a survey that said that consumers spend $150 billion on chocolate gifts each year, so this would be a great market to enter. And since this company already has a great reputation in the mail-order gift industry and the systems in place to handle the addition of this product, this would be a natural expansion of Perfect Posies' product line.*

This is a well-thought-out answer based on this candidate's knowledge of the company and the gift industry in general.

 Describe our competitors as you see them.

*How to **answer** it: As far as I can tell, your competitors have tried to branch out too often and too fast. They have tried to improve upon their main product, and with little success. As a result, they have had a lot of difficulty maintaining a consistent quality. I think that the recent bankruptcy of ABC Company only further illustrates this point. Your company has been smart enough to refrain from looking toward this same type of expansion and instead has focused on creating the best possible product. It is this kind of dedication that I am looking for in an employer.*

In addition to researching the company extensively, make sure you have a good idea of its competitors and what they do. Know in which areas the competition is beating out this company and in which they are lagging behind. Give evidence that in addition to a vast knowledge of the company, you know a lot about the industry as a whole. Most importantly, discuss how this company's initiatives are better suited to your personal interests.

 What do you think our distinct advantage is over our competitors?

*How to **answer** it: I think the smartest way to stay ahead of the industry was your choice of headquarters location. By operating in a low-cost area and maintaining a low production cost, you are able to spend aggressively on more important aspects, such as research and development and advertising. Even when the rest of the industry is showing a dip in sales, your company remains profitable.*

Again, this is the time to highlight your in-depth knowledge of the company, its products, and its operation in general. What things do you think the company does well, particularly when compared to their competitors? Pick one important aspect you see as a real advantage, and discuss it in an informed and intelligent manner.

 What do you think of our newest advertising campaign?

*How to **answer** it: If you are talking about the one with the family at breakfast time, I think it is great. I know that in the past your company has been criticized for offering foods that are high in fat. This comforting campaign—and the new heart-healthy product—was a great way to step away from that issue. It really shows that you care about your customers and take their comments and concerns seriously.*

Make sure to familiarize yourself with the company's latest happenings, including new products, new advertising campaigns, and any recent press (whether bad or good). Know enough about the company's current state to speak in an informed and intelligent manner. Always offer positive comments and make specific suggestions if you think they apply.

Q: Where do you think we're the most vulnerable as a business?

*How to **answer** it: The last company I worked for underwent a merger. Based on your cash position and strong product presence, your company would be an attractive target for a takeover. Though we did experience some difficulties in my last company, I also know I can weather the storm of such an occurrence.*

Answering this question requires a relatively strong grasp on the business and a definite knowledge of the firm's competitors. Figure out what the company does not do well in relation to its competitors, and talk a bit about this. Discuss how you would cope if these vulnerabilities were to be fully realized. As an employee with a passion for the business, you should always be thinking of the future of your job.

Q: If you were allowed to run the company, what would you do differently?

*How to **answer** it: I might investigate whether to sell off the light-manufacturing businesses and start an aggressive supplier-relations program.*

This is another question in which you must avoid stepping on anyone's toes. For example, if you are being interviewed by the human resources director, you probably wouldn't want to say, "I would change the overall structure of the human resources department. The way you are structured right now I'm surprised anyone gets hired." Rather than concentrate on your own personal experience, look at the company from a business standpoint. To answer this question, it really helps to have some insider information.

If you know people who work for the company—or even in the industry—see if they can help you. Make sure you keep the rules of business in mind. Companies don't turn a profit by letting their employees run wild. Keep your changes informed and intelligent; again, this is not the land of make-believe.

 Where do you think this company is going to be in five years?

*How to **answer** it: Based on what I've been reading, it seems this company will be fully expanded into the international market by then. Parker Corporation opened offices in Japan and Switzerland last year, and I read that they are looking into opening Canadian offices next year.*

This candidate is aware of what his prospective employer has in store for the future because he did his homework.

 How well do you understand our mission?

*How to **answer** it: From my research, I understand that your mission is to develop high-quality toys that enhance learning and provide entertainment for children between preschool age and ten years old.*

This candidate states the company's mission as she understands it, which is exactly what the interviewer asked her to do.

 If you were interviewing potential employees for a job here, how would you describe this organization to them?

*How to **answer** it: XRT, Inc., manufacturers windows and sells them directly to the consumer. The company has a sales force of about twenty people who respond to customer inquiries by visiting their homes or places of business.*

This answer shows that this interviewee has a firm grasp of what this business is all about.

Why You Want to Work Here

Q: **What makes you think you'd be particularly good at this job?**

How to **answer** *it: My academic career included several classes in business and marketing. Additionally, in my current internship, I have frequently been given the chance to help promote our products by attending trade shows, helping in the development of flyers and sales catalogs, and sitting in on meetings with the company sales department. I have been commended for my willingness to voice opinions and offer new ideas on how we could better market our products. I am forward thinking, and I always try to keep up with current trends. I think that my creativity and strong writing skills would augment the success I could have as part of your marketing team.*

The question is specifically asking about which skills and characteristics you possess that could help you succeed. Think about the kind of person that would be perfectly compatible with the job you are applying for. What skills do you possess that reflect this "perfect candidate"? Discuss how you keep up with the industry. Read the trade magazines and visit various organizational meetings and websites to find out about current trends. Make it part of your job to keep current, and make sure the interviewer knows that you are doing this.

Q: **Why do you want to work here?**

How to **answer** *it: About a year ago, your company beat me out for a bid on a project. To find out why the organization* *decided in your favor, I decided to research your products. It was then that I discovered that while many products in the computer industry are becoming increasingly similar, your company strives to be forward thinking. Since then, I have kept a very active interest in your company and the steps they have made in the industry as a whole. Your company has maintained a consistently strong service record, and your customer support is unrivaled. I believe that while many bigger companies will come and go, this company will always remain dedicated to the customer. I respect that kind of personal attention, and it's a characteristic that—unfortunately—is hard to find.*

All aspects of the interviewing company should come into play here. In addition to the actual business, you should talk about the other reasons why you would like to become a part of this particular company. For example, if you are applying to work in an office with just three or four employees, you could mention your preference for small companies. Tell the recruiter about the many reasons that made you apply for this position. If you don't know much about the company culture, look at aspects such as the company's reputation or the job description itself to help you come up with an answer. Customer feedback can also be of value in answering this question.

🗨 Why are you leaving your current job?

*How to **answer** it: Though at one point I made the leap from being a bank lender to working in the human resources department, I am hoping to combine these two experiences. Sure, I can work in human resources anywhere, but because of my past experience as a lender, I think that my skills would be well suited to a human resources career within your bank. As I have been on both sides of the traditional job interview, I think I have a strong ability to find those applicants who are most compatible with the job.*

Give two or three reasons why you are ready to leave your current job. Focus on discussing the lack of growth or responsibility in your current job, and how you think this new job will challenge you. Regardless of your feelings for your current boss or work environment, refrain from making any negative statements about either. Speaking disparagingly of your current job is a red flag to the interviewer that you could have an attitude problem. Your boss isn't there to defend herself, so the interviewer is left to wonder which one of you is the guilty party in all of this.

💬 What are you hoping to get out of your next job?

*How to **answer** it: I'd be very interested in taking control of a segment of the company in which we are really lagging behind. Sure, it would be a challenge, but that's exactly what I'm looking for. In my current position, I have been able to increase the sales in my territory by more than 30 percent in just a few years. If given the opportunity to work with your company, I believe I could do that again. I also hope to get a very aggressive commission structure if I'm able to turn around a problem territory.*

This question is very similar to the one that asks, "Why are you ready to leave your current job?" Without being negative about your current job or boss, give one or two examples of your current work experience that explain why you are interested in a new position. For this question, it is best to focus on obtaining a greater challenge. For example, telling the interviewer that there is no potential for advancement in your current position conveys that you are a hard worker who wants to advance; it also implies that you have gone as high as you can go in your current position. Make sure you give some reasons why you believe the job at hand will provide the additional responsibilities you are seeking.

Q: What would your dream job be like?

How to answer it: My dream job would allow me to be creative and artistic on a day-to-day basis. It would be fast paced and deadline driven, as I thrive on pressure. I would like to work for a small start-up company with limitless growth potential. I would like to be part of a company from the beginning so that I could help in the shaping of a new business. I know that your company has been around for about a year now, but I think that your potential for growth is endless. The reason I am so interested in this position is that it would allow me to do all of these things, and then some.

This is another question that might tempt you to offer up a bit of your fantasy life to the interviewer. Don't! Talk about a job you would like to have that either is close to or involves the same skills as the job you are applying for. Rather than cite a specific job title, your best bet is to tell the interviewer the tasks that would be involved in your dream job, and how those tasks relate to this job. Tie in the industry, size of the company, or other factors where appropriate.

Q: What motivates you to do this kind of work?

How to answer it: I have been fortunate enough in my schooling to have encountered many wonderful teachers. Each of them has left an indelible mark on me in some way, and I have always longed to do the same for some other child. I want to be the kind of teacher who not only encourages kids to learn but also sets an example that makes others want to teach. The quality of education in this state has been criticized over the past several years, and I want to help change this negative perception.

Here is a great opportunity to show your enthusiasm for an industry as well as your belief in the products or services of the company.

It is always a wise idea to use personal experiences to underscore your enthusiasm. Talk about your natural interests, as the interviewer is trying to find out if they are compatible with the job.

Q: **What interests you most about this job?**

> *How to **answer** it:* I would love the opportunity to work under Jane Doe, a woman who really helped to build the financial services practice under bank deregulation. I have worked closely with Ms. Doe on projects before, and I completely respect her and her opinions. I think that in addition to getting along with your boss, it is important to respect that person, and to believe in her. My esteem for Ms. Doe is one of the main reasons I chose to apply for this job.

Point out the new responsibilities you'll be assuming in this job, as well as the reasons why you are already well suited for it. Mention similarities to some of your past jobs in which you have enjoyed professional success. Do not speak in generalities!

In this case, the interviewee mentioned the name of someone at the company with whom she once enjoyed working. When mentioning a current employee's name at the company where you're interviewing, be sure to give his or her full name first, and then refer to the person as "Ms. Doe" or "Mr. Doe." The interviewer may think you're trying to be too familiar if you use the person's first name only. That can be off-putting to some people. So keep it professional and remember that this is a business meeting—not a chance to make friends with the interviewer.

Q: **What would you like to accomplish in this job that you weren't able to accomplish in your current position?**

> *How to **answer** it:* The company that I work for right now is rather small. That said, the budget we had for marketing our products was fairly limited. For the most part, our marketing efforts were limited to print ads and other traditional

resources. I know that your company dedicates much of its time and energy to interactive media, targeting the eighteen-to-twenty-five-year-old category. This is a step that I am looking forward to taking, and it's one that I think I have many good ideas for.

Answer here in the same way you'd answer the question, Why are you ready to leave your current job? Don't say anything negative, and be sure your answer reflects professional goals! Talk about the goals you have set for yourself and how this job would help you attain them. Discuss the things you enjoy and have an aptitude for, but do not dwell on the limitations imposed by your current or previous job.

What Your Career Plans Are

Q: Where do you see yourself in five years?

How to answer it: I would like to think that in five years I could be managing my own department within the company. As I have served directly under department heads in the past, I think that I have learned valuable lessons as to what it takes to be a good leader. I would like to have the chance to use these skills and, I hope, to make a difference within the company.

Here's one instance in which you don't want your answer to be too specific. If you think you would like to see yourself at a management level, say so, but refrain from giving an exact job title such as senior vice president of financial affairs. Showing that you are achievement motivated is one thing; telling the interviewer that you are out to get others fired is another. Use this question as a way to talk about your greatest skills. Again, be realistic. If you are being hired for the mailroom, it is unlikely that you will be running the show within the next five years.

Though confidence and a desire to be promoted are all valuable to an employer, an employee who is living in his or her own fixed reality is another story. One way to surely eliminate yourself from consideration for a job is to state unrelated career goals. If you're applying for a job as an accountant, it is not wise to tell the interviewer that in five years you hope to be the host of your own late-night talk show!

Q: **What other firms are you interviewing with, and for what positions?**

> *How to* **answer** *it: Since I have definitely decided on a career in the publishing industry, I am applying strictly for editorial assistant positions. My most recent interviews have been with some of the top publishing houses in this market.*

One mistake that interviewees often make is trying to impress the interviewer with the names of big companies. As each of the *Fortune* 500 businesses are unrelated as far as industry is concerned, this would be a mass mailing at its worst. Make sure the companies you mention are all within the same industry as the company you are interviewing with. Don't be afraid to tell the recruiter that you are interviewing with one of the company's biggest competitors. If anything, it will reinforce that this is exactly the kind of business you want to get into and illustrate that you're committed to finding a job in your field of interest, thus showing you to be a low-risk hire.

Q: **What would you say if one of our competitors offered you a position?**

> *How to* **answer** *it: I'd probably say no. I'm not too interested in working for the other players in this industry. My desire to work for Nike comes from the many positive experiences I have had with your product. I truly believe in your products and would not consider working for a company whose products I*

*didn't believe in. After all, how could I convince someone to
buy a product that I myself wouldn't buy?*

It is not always necessary to answer no to this question. Depending on the order of the questions asked, you may have already told
an interviewer that you are applying for a position with his competitor. Still, whether you answer this question with a yes or a no,
be sure that you let the interviewer know that it is this company
you would like to work for. Point out the reasons why you would
prefer to work for this company even if a competitor offered you a
position. Talk about the advantages this company has to offer you
both as an employee and as a consumer. Again, the interviewer
is trying to determine whether your interest in the company and
industry is genuine. Talk about why you would choose this company over any other, and demonstrate your interest.

**Q: How have your career motivations changed over the
past few years?**

*How to **answer** it: When I first started out, I worked in sales,
which is where I was sure I wanted to be. As I worked very
closely with the marketing department, I realized that perhaps that was where my talents were. I found out that I could
use my creativity and strong writing skills to really help out
in the marketing end of things. My boss also quickly realized this and immediately offered me a position within the
marketing department. Since then, my interest in marketing
has only increased. I know that your sales and marketing
departments rely heavily upon one another to make each
other work, as is the case with many companies. Though I
will always love the thrill of salesmanship, I cannot deny that
marketing is where I need to be. Working for your company
would allow me to keep a close eye on both of these interests and, I hope, help in the productivity of each of these
departments.*

Regardless of whether or not you have changed careers completely, you have probably learned a lot about yourself and your talents since entering the work force. Talk about the things that you have learned from your past work experience, especially where your skills and natural instincts lie. Make sure that your current motivation relates to the job you are interviewing for. Avoid seeming fickle. An employer will not want to take a chance on an employee who can't seem to make up his mind about what he wants to do. Even if you've had various jobs, talking about the goal you have always had in mind will put a positive spin on your varied past.

Q: **You seem to be climbing the corporate ladder in your current job. Why leave now?**

How to answer it: I'm choosing to leave now because my goals have changed. I want to use my public relations skills at a nonprofit organization such as this one.

This applicant is making a change to another industry, but shows how he can still use his skills to meet his new goals.

Q: **Your last job was very different than the ones you had before. Why did you take that job?**

How to answer it: I was thinking of going back to school to be a veterinarian. I mentioned this to my neighbor, a vet, and he offered me a job in his office. I love animals, but before I made the commitment to go to veterinary school, I wanted to make sure I'd be happy working with them and especially dealing with sick ones. It turned out that wasn't right for me after all.

This candidate has a good explanation for why she took a job that has nothing at all to do with her current career path. In doing so she also shows off her decision-making skills.

Describe how your career progressed over the past five years. Was it aligned with the goals you set for yourself?

*How to **answer** it: When I graduated from the community college, I knew I wanted to work as a store manager. I also knew I would have to work my way up, so I took a job as a sales associate at Dress Corral. After a lot of hard work, I was promoted to assistant department manager after two years. After being in that job for a year, I got a job as manager of the ladies' accessories department at P. J. Coopers, and I've been there for the past two years. With my experience, I'm ready for the next step—store manager.*

This job candidate shows exactly how her career has progressed and how she is now ready for a job with this employer.

 How does this job fit in with your career goals?

*How to **answer** it: As I mentioned earlier, my long-range goal is to be an elementary school principal. Reaching that is several years off, of course. I have a lot to learn about school administration. I've attended several workshops you've run, and I am always impressed by your knowledge, and I know I can learn a lot from you. From what I've heard through the grapevine, you always place a lot of trust in everyone you hire and give employees a chance to grow. I know I can gain valuable knowledge and experience here at Oakwood, in addition to what I can contribute as an assistant principal.*

This candidate demonstrates her knowledge about her prospective employer. She has personally learned from him in the past. She has also talked to other people who know him and how the school is run.

How You Would Contribute

Q: How do you stay current?

*How to **answer** it:* *I pore over the* Wall Street Journal, *the* New York Times, Institutional Investor, *and several mutual fund newsletters. I also have a number of friends who are financial analysts, and we often discuss the business amongst ourselves.*

This question relates to the previous one. Show the employer that your interest in a specific job or field does not end at 5 p.m. Talk about the many ways that—even outside of work—you keep up with your business. It could be that you spend your lazy Sunday mornings reading trade magazines; there's no shame in sharing this with the interviewer. If you are a member of any professional trade organization, now is the time to talk about it. Do you attend regular meetings or chat frequently with the other members? Show the employer that this position is not just a way to make a living but a way of life for you.

Q: Tell me something about yourself that I wouldn't know from reading your resume.

*How to **answer** it:* *I love snorkeling. It's my favorite way to relax. Down there, observing all those strange and wonderful forms of life, it gives a fresh and upbeat outlook on my own life.*

Remember that you are being asked to tell the interviewer something about yourself that she wouldn't know from reading your resume. If certain pieces of information were omitted from your resume to keep it all on one page, now is the time to bring them up. For example, if in addition to a part-time job and your full-time studies you were part of an athletic team or organization, talk about it. While the actual organization might be a bit off the topic, you can usually find a way to weave it into the conversation. By participating in a particular event or becoming part of a certain organization, what did you learn? What are some of the skills you acquired that will help you in your professional endeavors? Do not tell the interviewer something that is completely irrelevant (such as, "I have ten cats!"). Above all, remember not to repeat anything that can be found from looking at your resume.

Q: Do you think that you are overqualified for this position?

*How to **answer** it: Absolutely not! My relative experience and qualifications will only help me to do this job better. Because I have experience in so many different facets of your business, I feel that I can help in the overall success of the company, and not just within my department. For example, my business experience can help me to run the art department in a cost-efficient manner, while my creative background will allow me to find the best freelance talent. As I have been working in the industry for quite some time, I have many business contacts that I can call upon to help me. My qualifications are better for the company, too, since you'll be getting a better return on your investment. Since I am interested in establishing a long-term relationship with my employer, I would expect expanded responsibilities that could even make use of other skills when I have proven myself.*

This question intends to catch an interviewee off guard, and it often does. The mistake many people make in answering this question is to automatically take a defensive position. If you do have extensive experience, an interviewer is testing to see whether you would quickly become bored in the position, how much confidence you have in your own skills, and how you plan to let your past experience work for you in this company. When answering this question, be sure to address each of your strongest skills and explain how each could benefit the company. Confidence is the key to answering this question.

 What new or unique skills could you bring to the job that other candidates aren't likely to offer?

*How to **answer** it: Because the company I currently work for is one of the oldest players in the industry, I think I could bring the history and experience that goes along with that. I can help this company avoid making some of the same mistakes we have made in our established markets. For example, if I were to start work today, I would work at retaining your core customer base before trying to secure new accounts. It is this kind of experience that you are not likely to find in many other candidates.*

This question addresses your desire to add true value to a job (beyond what is expected of an employee). Imagine that you are being considered for the position alongside one other person with the exact same educational and professional qualifications. What are the things that would make you the better hire? Steer clear of vague answers such as "I am multitask oriented" and "I wear many hats." These answers tell the recruiter absolutely nothing about your skills and abilities.

 Based on what you know about this company, how will you contribute to it?

*How to **answer** it: I see that most of your company's clients are in the food industry. Since I spent ten years working for AMJ Bean Company, I am very familiar with that industry. I know my experience in the industry is something your clients will appreciate.*

This candidate has researched her prospective employer and knows that her experience in the food industry will help her should she be hired. She is able to make a point of mentioning that in the job interview.

 Do you know what your job duties will be if we hire you?

*How to **answer** it: As eligibility clerk, I know I will use my interviewing skills to help determine whether individuals are eligible to receive assistance from various government programs. I will interview people and then write reports that will be sent to the appropriate agencies.*

This candidate knows what the general duties are for the job.

 What would you like to accomplish here if we hire you?

*How to **answer** it: I read that this company is expanding into the children's clothing market. With my background in that area, I know I can help make that clothing line successful.*

The interviewee bases his answer on what he has learned about this employer. He explains how his experience will help the company reach its goals.

 If you were hired here today, what is the first thing you would do?

*How to **answer** it: I would help to increase your business within the software market. Though your company is mainly known for its printed products, I believe that your software is one of your greatest assets. I have spent the past four years working as a sales manager for a software developer, so I have a great understanding of how to market these products more effectively.*

In addition to showing your enthusiasm for a job, this question tests your knowledge of a company and its products. Give the interviewer clear, tangible evidence that the company will benefit immediately upon hiring you. Focus your answer on the action you would take, and—above all—make sure your goals are realistic. Is there an area you think could use some improvement? Discuss the steps you would take to achieve maximum results. Do you have a creative way to improve some aspect of the company? Talk about it. If you can, relate what you would like to accomplish in this company to past achievements and experience. A job offer is a cause to celebrate, but the interviewer isn't probing for that kind of response; she wants to know how you can make a difference right from day one.

 Our latest venture has been all over the news. What would you do to make the transition go more smoothly for our employees?

*How to **answer** it: I would make sure employees know how the merger between this company and Pacific Pencil Company will affect them. I would hold meetings to discuss how procedures will change and schedule workshops to help employees adapt to these changes. When my former employer merged with RQR International, I assisted the vice president who was responsible for handling the transition, so I have experience in this area.*

By referring to the venture by name, this candidate shows he knows what the interviewer is talking about. He has clearly given some thought to how this merger will affect the company and knows how to deal with it, and he can draw upon his experience with a similar situation.

Why should we hire you?

*How to **answer** it: My aunt had a company that was a small-scale manufacturer in the industry, and although she later sold the business, I worked there for five summers doing all sorts of odd jobs. For that reason, I believe*

I know this business from the ground up, and you can be assured that I know what I'd be getting into as a plant manager here.

Why *should* a company hire you? This question, which is usually the last one asked in a formal interview, is your chance to sum up your skills and value as an employee *without* repeating your resume or employment history. Here's your chance to offer one or two examples that explain why you want to work for this particular company and why they would want you to work for them. What's the most compelling example you can give to prove your interest? Though this question often remains unasked, it's always in the back of a recruiter's mind. If you're lucky enough to get through the interview without hearing it, you should still try to find an opportunity to use your prepared response sometime during the interview, perhaps in your closing remarks.

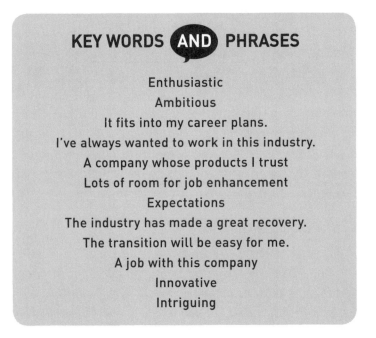

KEY WORDS AND PHRASES

Enthusiastic

Ambitious

It fits into my career plans.

I've always wanted to work in this industry.

A company whose products I trust

Lots of room for job enhancement

Expectations

The industry has made a great recovery.

The transition will be easy for me.

A job with this company

Innovative

Intriguing

Major clients
I look for your label/brand/logo.
Consistent quality
Best possible product
Dedication
Low production cost
Care about your customers
Strong grasp of the business
Competitors
Expand your market
The company's mission
Offer new ideas
Keep up with new trends
Combine my experiences
I'm looking for challenges.
Fast-paced and deadline-driven
I thrive on pressure.
Wonderful teacher
Perception
I would love to work with . . .
It is important to respect my boss.
Goals I've set
Things I enjoy and have aptitude for
I believe in your products.
Advantages this company has to offer
Why I would choose this company
My past work experience
My goals have changed.
Commitment
I'm ready for the next step.
I've attended your workshops.
Valuable knowledge and experience
My experience will help me do the job better.

Better return on your investment
Long-term relationship with my employer
I know this business from the ground up.
I am familiar with this industry.
My knowledge of the company and its products

Chapter 7

Providing **Details** about Your **Education**

WHEN PROSPECTIVE EMPLOYERS INTERVIEW RECENT GRADUATES WITHOUT MUCH experience, they can learn a lot about applicants by asking questions about their school experience. Therefore, if you're interviewing for jobs straight out of school, you should be prepared to answer a lot of questions about your education. The interviewer will want to know about your performance as a student, how you felt about particular subjects, which teachers you liked and why. If you did an internship, be prepared to discuss that experience in detail. The interviewer will want to know what you learned there and what contributions you made. The interviewer will want to know about your extracurricular activities, too. All of this information lets her get a better look at who you are.

Why You Chose Your Major

Q: **I see you majored in English. Are you prepared for a job in marketing and sales?**

*How to **answer** it: As an English major, I had to do a large amount of reading and needed to retain all of it. Reading and absorbing the literature on the products I'll be selling will be* *a snap. I believe college also prepared me to manage my time well. I have hands-on experience in this field as well; I worked in various sales positions to put myself through school.*

Notice that the interviewee doesn't make any excuses for working in a field outside his major. Instead, he talks about how his major qualifies him for this job. He also talks about the fact that he has sales experience.

 Why did you choose to major in philosophy?

*How to **answer** it: From a very early age, I wanted to be a lawyer. When I started to do my research, I found out that undergraduates who want to go to law school should take a lot of liberal arts classes. During my freshman year, I took different courses in the school of liberal arts and sciences, and I liked philosophy the best, so I decided to make it my concentration.*

This applicant shows that she made an informed choice when choosing her major.

 What was your favorite subject in high school? What was your favorite subject in college?

*How to **answer** it: English was my favorite subject in high school. I did a lot of writing in English. I liked working hard to put together a paper and then getting feedback in the form of a grade. My favorite classes in college were those in my major. I actually took only one marketing class before I declared marketing as my major. I found the subject matter so interesting that I started looking into it as a career choice.*

This candidate explains why English was her favorite subject and in the process demonstrates her skill as a writer, which she knows will be an important part of her job. By stating that her major was her favorite subject in college, she shows that she is dedicated to the field.

 What were your least favorite subjects in high school and college?

How to answer it: My least favorite subject in high school was home economics. I helped with the housekeeping at home; I didn't want to have to deal with it at school, too. I liked most of the classes I took in college. If I had to pick my least favorite, I guess it would have to be biology. We had to dissect a fetal pig, and I had a problem doing that.

The candidate picked classes unrelated to the job he's applying for. Notice also that he didn't say he disliked the classes because of their difficulty.

 Why did you decide to major in elementary education?

How to answer it: When I was in high school, I took an assessment test to help me figure out what career I should go into. When I got my results, teaching was one of the occupations on the list, along with several others like psychology, social work, and nursing. When I started researching the occupations in more detail, I discovered that teaching was the one that appealed to me most.

This candidate put a lot of thought into choosing an occupation. This answer not only shows her dedication to teaching but also that she makes decisions carefully.

 Are you planning to get your MBA?

How to answer it: I would like to do that. I'm trying to find a program with a schedule that won't interfere with work.

This interviewee knows that an MBA is highly valued in her field, but she anticipates that her potential employer might be concerned that her work schedule would be compromised if she pursues one. She heads off those fears.

Why You Chose Your School

Q: **Why did you choose Adams University?**

*How to **answer** it: Adams University has an accredited business school. It is ranked third in the nation. The university also has a great cross-country team, and I wanted to try out for it.*

This candidate put a lot of thought into choosing a college, implying that's how she makes all her decisions. She also uses this opportunity to brag about the quality of her education.

Q: **I see you transferred to Hamford University from Sannau County Community College. Why did you start at a two-year school?**

*How to **answer** it: I knew I wanted to earn a bachelor's degree. I also wanted to go to Hamford, but the cost of a four-year education there was extremely high. I decided to take my core classes at a community college to save money. I first checked to make sure Hamford would take my credits. Since Sannau is a very well respected community college, I knew I would get a decent education there.*

By giving this answer, the interviewee demonstrates that she is a very practical person. She spends money wisely but doesn't compromise her goals. She also doesn't do something without first investigating it.

Q: Why did you choose to go away to college rather than going to one near your home?

How to answer it: I wanted to be responsible for myself, and I knew that wouldn't happen at home. By living in the dorms, I had no choice but to manage my own time, budget my money, and set my own limits.

This candidate saw going away to college as a learning experience, both in and out of the classroom.

Courses You Took and Grades

Q: I see you majored in marketing. What courses did you take outside your major?

How to answer it: I took a few psych classes because I felt that knowing how people think would be to my advantage in marketing. I took some art classes because I really enjoy that. I also took writing courses because I thought that was an important skill to have.

Instead of just giving a list of courses, this candidate talks about why she took them and how two of the subjects will help in her career.

Q: I see it took you four and a half years to graduate. Can you explain that?

How to answer it: I had a difficult time adjusting during my freshman year. I wasn't quite ready for all the demands of college. I had to take a few classes over. During the summer between my freshman and sophomore years, I went to a few workshops to help me improve my study skills and my time management skills. By the time I was a sophomore, I was a much more serious student.

This candidate doesn't make excuses for his failings, but rather speaks about how he overcame them and how he succeeded in the end.

 What grade did you receive in your favorite class?

*How to **answer** it: My favorite class was Intro to Journalism. It was actually pretty tough at first. Everything I handed in came back marked up in red ink. I must have gotten D's on the first four assignments. There were a few times that I found just the right words to capture an event, though, and I loved that feeling, so I stuck with it. Fortunately my professor gave us the opportunity to redo our work for a higher grade, and although it took some extra work, ultimately I got an A in the class.*

It's easy to like a class if you don't have to work hard for a good grade. This applicant explains why journalism was her favorite class despite having to work hard.

Never say: "Intro to Journalism. I got an A." Without saying more than that, the interviewer is left to wonder whether the candidate liked that class simply because she got an A in it.

 What grade did you receive in your least favorite class?

*How to **answer** it: My least favorite class was Art History. I know other people who took the class with other professors, got a C, and loved it. I hated the class and got an A. I didn't learn anything. I just had to show up for every class.*

Clearly this candidate likes to work hard and isn't impressed with getting rewarded for "just showing up."

 What courses best prepared you for this job?

*How to **answer** it: I took a course in research and bibliographic methods that provided me with the technical skills to*

do this job. The most important thing I learned in that class was that there is a resource available to answer almost all questions. I also took several classes in children's and young adult literature. I saw from the job description that the person who takes this position will also have to spend several hours a week in the children's department.

This candidate not only lists some courses he took, but also explains how they will help him do the job should he be hired.

 What elective accounting courses did you take?

*How to **answer** it: I took three auditing classes because I knew I wanted to work in public accounting. I also took an international accounting class. In this global economy, I knew that would come in handy at some point in my career.*

This candidate explains how she chose courses she would be able to use professionally.

 Your GPA wasn't very high. Can you please explain that?

*How to **answer** it: During my first two years of college, I was kind of immature and didn't work hard enough. I worked really hard my junior and senior years, but unfortunately those first two years really brought down my GPA. It was hard to recover from that.*

This candidate acknowledges that he was responsible for his low GPA, but also talks about how he worked hard to raise it.

 Why weren't your grades better in school?

*How to **answer** it: School was a wonderful experience for me. I really enjoyed learning new ideas, I studied consistently, and I was attentive in class. But I never believed in cramming the night before an exam just to get a higher grade or staying*

up all night to finish a term paper. I really believe I learned just as much as many students who went for the grades.

If you've made it to the interview stage, it is likely that your qualifications meet what the employer is looking for. In this case, the interviewer is just interested in how you react to her inquiry. The most important thing in responding to this question is not to get defensive or place blame on someone else. Instead, try to put a positive spin on it. For example, you could focus your answer on what you learned and the extra effort you put in to learning, rather than on the actual grades you received. Be aware that your grades could be just fine; don't take this question personally and don't think it is an insult in any way.

Extracurricular Activities and Internships

 What extracurricular activities did you participate in?

*How to **answer** it: During my junior year of college, I was president of the psychology club. Then in my senior year, I was editor of the yearbook. I wrote for both my high school and college newspapers, too.*

This candidate highlights his leadership experience. He also calls attention to a very important skill—writing.

 Why didn't you participate more in extracurricular activities?

*How to **answer** it: I wanted to give as much effort as possible to my studies. Though I had done very well in high school, I lived in a very small town, and the school didn't prepare me very well for college. To keep getting the A's I had become accustomed to, I was forced to study very hard. Luckily, I was able to grasp material quickly enough that I found time to*

explore the city and make new friends. Still, between studying, working a part-time job, and socializing with friends, I never had much time for organized, extracurricular activities.

The interviewer is a bit concerned that you don't have many outside interests and, therefore, that you may eventually suffer from burnout. Employers like candidates who are well rounded and have interests outside of work. If you didn't participate in formal extracurricular activities in college, you still may want to talk about some of your interests, such as reading or exercising, that you participated in on a more informal level. For instance, you may have a passion for running, even if you weren't on the college track team.

Q: **I see you had an internship in this field. What did you learn from it?**

*How to **answer** it: My internship at Carlson Corporate allowed me to get some hands-on experience in this field that I wouldn't have gotten in classes alone. I learned that jobs in this field are often stressful, and long hours are often required. On the other hand, I got to find out how wonderful it is when you're on a team that helps land a big account as a result of hard work.*

This applicant speaks about what he gained from the internship and what he learned about the positive and negative aspects of working in the field.

Q: **Why haven't you done any internships?**

*How to **answer** it: I would have loved to have done an internship, but unfortunately I had to work my way through college. Most internships don't pay that well. However, as you can see from my resume, I made a point of finding work within this industry. Even though I was in the mailroom, I was still exposed to the field.*

While internships are important, sometimes extenuating circumstances get in the way. This candidate has no choice but to be honest about that. However, she explains how she tried to make up for not being able to do an internship.

 How did you spend your summers during college?

*How to **answer** it: I worked every summer to earn money for books and part of my tuition. I had this great job at a day camp. I started off as a counselor the summer before my senior year of high school, moved up to group leader the summer after I graduated, and then became assistant director.*

This applicant takes the opportunity to show off a little. He stayed at the same job for several years and was promoted to a supervisory position.

What You Gained from Your College Experience

 Did you have any teachers who influenced you?

*How to **answer** it: Yes, I did. It goes all the way back to junior high school. Mr. Danzer was my earth science teacher. He loved the subject, and he loved teaching. I think both these things came across in his ability to teach. It showed me that if a person loves what he does, he's more likely to excel at it. That was good to know when it came time to choose a career.*

This candidate tells which teacher influenced him and how.

 What did you gain from attending college?

*How to **answer** it: I gained knowledge about this field. I was able to use what I learned in class on the internship I did last summer at the Tallahassee Tribune. College is where I learned to be independent. There wasn't anyone pushing me*

to complete assignments on time, so I had to learn how to manage my time well and stay organized.

This candidate talks about things he learned both in and out of the classroom. He includes technical skills as well as soft skills— time management and organization.

 Aside from coursework, what was the most enriching part of your college education?

*How to **answer** it: I was very involved on the programming committee. As a matter of fact, I was chair during my senior year. We were responsible for planning on-campus events for the student body. The goal was to hold events that were well attended and safe. That meant hiring entertainment that appealed to the majority of students and making sure campus security was present to enforce the rules.*

This applicant talks about her work on this committee as if it were a job. She explains her goals and how she met them.

 What would your professors say about you?

*How to **answer** it: My professors would say I always turned in high-quality work. They would say I contributed to classroom discussions by offering interesting comments and asking good questions. They would also say I was willing to help other students.*

This candidate takes the opportunity to highlight some positive attributes.

 Have you ever had a disagreement with a professor? How did you handle it?

*How to **answer** it: I disagreed about a grade I received once. I spent a lot of time researching and writing a paper for a*

history class. When I got the paper back with a B, I was very disappointed. After thinking about it for a day, I decided to talk to the professor. He asked me what grade I thought I deserved. I said I thought I had earned an A on the paper and explained why. He said he would read the paper over and regrade it if he found my arguments were valid. The next day he told me he changed my grade to an A.

This student knows how to stand up for herself when there is something she feels strongly about. She demonstrates how she persuaded her teacher to change her grade by presenting her arguments in a calm manner after waiting a day to collect her thoughts.

Q: **What was the most difficult assignment you had while in school?**

*How to **answer** it: I took a creative writing class. It was one of many electives I could choose. I had to write a poem. I discovered I'm not really good at that sort of thing.*

This interviewee chose to discuss an assignment that was entirely unrelated to his major and to anything he would be expected to do at this job.

Q: **What did you like most about college?**

*How to **answer** it: I really enjoyed playing on the volleyball team. During my freshman and sophomore years, we weren't as strong as we could have been. We pulled together, and by my junior year we were ranked number two in our division. By my senior year, we were ranked first place.*

This candidate's mention of her participation on an athletic team draws attention to her ability to work on a team. From her research, she knows employees of this company often work on teams.

Q: Why didn't you finish college?

*How to **answer** it: I left school because of financial reasons. My parents couldn't afford my tuition, so I decided to work for a few years. The experience was actually a great one for me. I learned a lot from it. I'm planning to take some classes next semester. I just heard about a great program that offers classes online. I checked the program out with the State Education Department, and it's legitimate.*

Dropping out of school for financial reasons is certainly acceptable. This candidate speaks positively of her work experience, claiming that she gained something from it. Her plan to take some classes won't affect her work schedule.

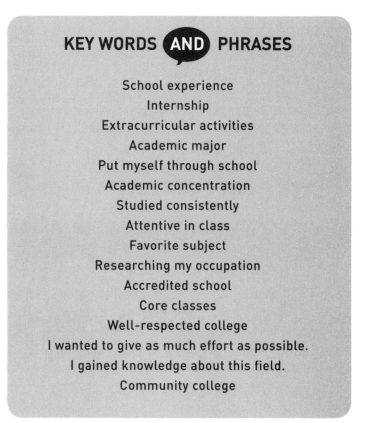

KEY WORDS **AND** PHRASES

School experience
Internship
Extracurricular activities
Academic major
Put myself through school
Academic concentration
Studied consistently
Attentive in class
Favorite subject
Researching my occupation
Accredited school
Core classes
Well-respected college
I wanted to give as much effort as possible.
I gained knowledge about this field.
Community college

Offering interesting comments
Manage my own time, budget, and limits
Technical skills
Grade point average
School was a wonderful experience.
New ideas
Well rounded
Interests outside of work
Teachers who influenced me
Enriching
Enjoyed
Electives
Worked very hard
Researching and writing class papers
Class outline

Chapter 8

Navigating Hard-to-Answer Questions

ONE FEAR EMBEDDED IN THE MIND OF EVERY INTERVIEWEE—AND RIGHTFULLY so—is the thought of being asked a question you don't know the answer to. The key to rising above these types of questions is to remain calm, cool, and confident in your answer. Be diplomatic and positive, no matter what you are asked.

Different questions will be asked of students and recent graduates as opposed to people who have been in the workforce for several years. Different responses will be anticipated from job applicants who are re-entering the market after a break or candidates who have been laid off. You may be asked to discuss your experience working with a difficult boss or explain why there are gaps in your resume. This chapter will help you be prepared for any question, no matter what your situation.

Discussing Frustrations and Failures

 Tell me about a project in which you were a bit disappointed in your own performance.

*How to **answer** it: In my last job with a manufacturing company, I had to analyze all the supplier bids and present*

recommendations to the vice president of logistics. Because the supplier bids weren't in a consistent format, my analysis often consisted of comparing dissimilar items. This caused some confusion in my final report, and by the time I'd reworked it and presented it to the vice president, we'd lost the critical time we'd needed to improve our approval process for these bids. In hindsight, I should have set the bid format so that we could assess similar items. Ever since, I've used a request for proposal process consistent with the results we are looking to achieve.

Describe the barriers you've come across in past experiences and how you've worked around them. How have your skills come into play? In hindsight, what could you have done differently? Most importantly, turn this roadblock into a lesson and tell the interviewer what you learned from having gone through the experience.

Q: Which aspects of your work are most often criticized?

*How to **answer** it: In my first job as marketing assistant, I spent endless hours analyzing a particular problem for which I knew there was a better solution. I came up with a revised marketing plan that was extremely well received by my coworkers. Unfortunately, when it came time to present the plan to the top-level management, I wasn't well versed in PowerPoint. My presentation was dull, and the proposal was turned down. I'd failed to effectively market and showcase the real benefits of my plan, such as the savings that would result from implementing it. I spent the next two weeks working on a presentation with a bit more sizzle, and on my second try, management approved it; my recommendations were carried out to everyone's satisfaction. I was very grateful to have been given that second chance. Since then, I certainly make sure that all the details have been taken care of* *when I am proposing something new to a group so that there are no questions left unanswered.*

Though the answer given here seems to skirt the issue a bit, that's okay. The best way to answer this question is to give an example of something you overlooked—or a mistake that you made—earlier in your career. Discuss the ways in which you worked to overcome the situation and to improve your work. Talk about how the failure has changed the way you work now, or how it has caused you to pay more careful attention to detail in all your work.

 Tell me about a situation that frustrated you at work.

*How to **answer** it: I was frustrated once when a client who had insisted on purchasing a high-growth stock called in a panic because the stock had dropped more than twenty points in one day. I had a hard time convincing her to ride it out rather than cut her losses. I think what frustrated me most was that this happened despite my attempts from the beginning to explain the short-term volatility of that stock.*

This is another question designed to probe the candidate's professional personality. The interviewer will want reassurance that you are able to withstand pressure on the job. Describe how you've remained diplomatic, objective, or professional in a difficult situation. Pick a situation in which, again, you will not raise any major doubts or concerns in the mind of the interviewer. Depict yourself as able to work through the problems that arise in any job with tact and no hard feelings.

Tell me about a time when your employer wasn't happy with your work performance.

*How to **answer** it: When I first began working as a paralegal, I handed in two letters with typos in them during my first week* *on the job. Perhaps my nervousness at beginning a new career contributed to my carelessness, but I soon learned to be an excellent proofreader. After that first week, my boss told me regularly how happy he was with my work.*

Talking about your role in causing a company to go bankrupt certainly will not win you any points here. Instead, try to think of a relatively minor incident in which you made a mistake but were able to learn from it. Also, show your willingness to accept responsibility for the problem; don't blame others or make excuses. Simply describe what happened and what you did to successfully resolve the situation. In the time since that incident, how have you redeemed yourself or improved upon your past mistakes?

Q: Give me an example of a time when you were asked to complete a task but weren't given enough information to get it done.

How to **answer** *it: At my first job as a publicity assistant, I was given the task of assembling 500 press kits for immediate mailing. The work had already been done, but I was unsure of whether or not there was a specific order in which each of the pages needed to be arranged. My supervisor had already left for a meeting, but I was able to track her down in her car. She explained to me the order in which the kits needed to be assembled, and the work was completed fairly quickly. In the end, I managed to prevent a problem that would have cost several hours of time to rectify, not to mention a bunch of headaches.*

In answering this question, you want to reassure the interviewer that you are mature and responsible enough to handle problems that are likely to occur. Think of a situation in which you were able to think quickly enough to prevent a problem. Talk about your own resourcefulness and initiative in getting the job done in a timely and professional manner.

Q: **Tell me about a time when you failed to resolve a conflict that had arisen.**

*How to **answer** it:* I wasn't able to keep a good employee who had been working in one of my company's manufacturing facilities for more than twenty years. As part of the company's modernization policy, all job descriptions were rewritten to require some sort of computer skills. Though I offered to pay the cost of classes so that he could gain these skills, he refused. Unfortunately, I had no other option than to replace him, as the new technology we were using required these skills. When I look back on the experience, I really wish I had been more vocal to him and the other employees about acquiring new training periodically. That way, when new techniques were introduced, he may not have been so overwhelmed. Now I am vigilant about encouraging those in my work group to attend seminars and training classes to enhance their job skills. I have even had various professionals come into the office and teach some classes on-site.

The best way to answer this question is to discuss a difficult situation but one that was not really yours to solve in the first place. Briefly introduce the problem, but focus more on the steps you took to solve the problem. What was the result of your work? What did you learn from the experience? How has that experience changed your professional behavior today?

Q: **How do you feel when things go wrong on a project? How do you handle it?**

*How to **answer** it:* Though I would obviously prefer that all of the projects I work on run smoothly, I am realistic enough to know that this cannot happen. This is especially true in

the case of the biotechnology industry, in which changes can and will happen to any plan at any time. I try to realize from the outset of any project that the plan we come up with is only the best-case scenario plan and that it may need to be changed at any given moment. When plans begin to unravel, my approach is just to cross each bridge when I come to it and not obsess about it beforehand. One of the ways in which I try to prepare for complications is to come up with some alternative plans. Though this does work in some cases, it doesn't help in all; sometimes you can't prepare for a problem until it's right there in front of you. My basic attitude is to take it all in stride.

This is a very tricky question. As the interviewee, you should understand that from the outset. What the interviewer is really trying to get at here is whether you have the ability to work under pressure. Without going into too much detail about all the projects that have somehow gone wrong in your professional history, reassure the interviewer that you can and do handle pressure with ease and professionalism.

Q: **Have you ever been passed up for a promotion you thought you deserved?**

*How to **answer** it: A couple times in my early career, I thought I was unfairly passed up for a promotion. However, in retrospect, I now realize that I probably wasn't ready to perform those jobs. In fact, the additional training I received remaining where I was proved invaluable in the last few years, as I've made significant progress moving up the corporate ladder. I've also learned to appreciate that being ready for a promotion doesn't necessarily mean it will happen. There are many external factors aside from a person's performance and capabilities that need to be taken into consideration.*

The interviewer wants to gauge the candidate's self-confidence and objectivity about personal or professional limitations. Be sure to give evidence here that you have enough patience to learn what is important before you get bored in one position or frustrated because you have not been promoted. After you've mastered your own job, would you stay motivated long enough to be productive? If you've never been passed up for a promotion—or if you've never been up for a promotion at all—it's okay to say so. Perhaps you've only been in the work force for a short period of time and don't think you've acquired strong enough skills to be promoted. Whatever the case, be honest.

 Tell me about your least favorite manager or professor.

*How to **answer** it: Well, I've been pretty fortunate as far as managers go, and I didn't have any problems with my professors. In my first job out of college, I worked with a manager who was pretty inaccessible. If you walked into her office to ask a question, you got the sense that you were bothering her, so my coworkers and I just learned to get help from each other instead. She was good in a lot of ways, but I would have preferred that she'd been more available to us and given us more direction.*

Answering this question will be a little bit like walking across a minefield, so be careful! Keep in mind that the interviewer doesn't really want to learn about your former supervisors but about the way you speak of them. Though the interviewer may bait you to make a negative statement about your former employer, doing so can create a host of problems. Even if your claim is completely true and entirely justified, the recruiter may conclude either that you don't get along well with people in general (or specifically with those in authority positions) or that you often shift blame to others. The best way around this dilemma is to choose an example that's not too negative, touch upon it briefly, then focus the rest of your answer on what you learned from the experience.

Q: **Who's the toughest employer you've ever had to work for and why?**

*How to **answer** it:* The most difficult employer I've ever had would definitely have to be Mr. Rogers at the Brady Project. He would push people to their limits when things got busy, and he was a stickler for detail. But he was always fair, and he always rewarded people when they worked hard and did a good job. I'd definitely call him a tough boss, but I'd also call him a good boss.

This question is another in which the interviewer is sort of daring you to make negative statements about a previous employer. Just remember that even the most difficult of bosses has taught you something new, so focus on that part of the experience. Turn the question around with a positive, upbeat response. Be sure to mention the positive aspects of this boss in addition to the qualities that made her so tough.

Q: **Have you ever had to work with a manager who you thought was unfair to you or who was just plain difficult to get along with?**

*How to **answer** it:* Fortunately, I've never really run into that problem. Of course, my current boss has to work under time constraints—just like everyone else—and she sometimes has a tendency to **answer** things rather bluntly to push our department to meet its goals. But I've never considered that unfair or hard to handle; it's just part of the job. My supervisors and I have always gotten along quite well.

Again, no matter how many times an interviewer gives you the opportunity to do so, never criticize a current or former employer!

The interviewer is not really interested in finding out whether or not you have worked for difficult people in the past; we all have. What he is trying to discover is whether or not (and how easily) you are willing to badmouth these people.

 What are some of the things your supervisor has done that you disliked?

*How to **answer** it: The only thing I really don't like is to get feedback in front of others. I want to hear good or bad feedback in private so that I have time to think and react to the issue without other distractions. I believe that's the fair way to improve learning or to change future behavior.*

Again, avoid being overly negative about your ex-boss or manager. Discuss a relatively minor example of one with which the interviewer is likely to empathize. Put a positive spin on your answer by describing what you learned from this difficult situation.

 Tell me about two or three aspects of your last job that you never want to repeat.

*How to **answer** it: One of the skills that I am most proud of is my fairly extensive background in credit collections; it has enabled me to make better risk assessments in my everyday job. Though I really enjoyed the experience I received from having worked in collections, it was not a job that I particularly enjoyed, and it isn't something that I would want to do again.*

In a completely constructive way, describe one or two things you've done that you didn't especially enjoy or that didn't play upon your greatest strengths. Though this question specifically targets a negative topic, it's easy to turn this around: After talking about why you didn't like a particular job or task, describe your strengths and their relevance to the job you're applying for.

Special Situations

Q: **You were at your last job for only six months. Why so short a time?**

*How to **answer** it: Unfortunately, the job turned out to be much different than what I thought it would be. Fortunately though, I found this out early on—before the employer invested more time in me and I invested more time in the company. I know I could put my editing skills to much better use in this position.*

Notice the interviewer places no blame on either herself or the employer. She doesn't say that the employer didn't tell her the truth about the job or that she misunderstood what she'd be doing. She also shows how she looked out for both her employer and herself by leaving before more time was invested.

Q: **I see from your resume that you've had five jobs in five years. Why have you moved around so much?**

*How to **answer** it: When I first graduated from college, I wasn't sure what I wanted to do. Five years later I'm committed to working in this field. I even took some courses to enhance my skills. I know I can do a good job here.*

This is an honest answer. The candidate states that she is now committed to the field and proves it by talking about classes she has taken.

Q: **Why did you stay in your last job for such a long time?**

*How to **answer** it: I was in my last job for more than seven years. During that time, I completed an advanced technical degree at an evening university and also had two six-month assignments in which I was loaned out to different* *departments. As a result, I acquired some additional skills that normally aren't associated with that job. Therefore, I think I've made good progress and am ready to accept the next challenge.*

An interviewer may also be curious as to why you would stay in one particular position for too long. If you've been with the same company for an extended time, the interviewer may be curious about your interest in personal improvement, tackling new assignments, and so on. He may also be concerned about whether you have a tendency to get too comfortable with the status quo. Demonstrate how you've developed job responsibilities in meaningful new ways in your many years on the job and that you are expecting to do the same with this company.

 Why do you want to leave your current position?

*How to **answer** it: My current position has allowed me to learn a great deal about the plastics industry, and I am very glad to have had that opportunity. However, I've also found that my interests really lie in research and development, which my company has recently decided to phase out over the next two years. That is why I am so interested in your organization. As I understand, your company places a great deal of importance on research and development and is also a highly respected leader in the industry.*

The interviewer's foremost concern with career changers will always be why they want to switch careers. But people do it every day, so don't think you will not get the job just because you don't have any hands-on experience in the field. Show the interviewer that your decision to switch careers has been based on careful consideration. Explain why you decided on this particular position and how the position will allow you to further your skills and interests.

Q: **Why would you want to leave an established career at an employment agency for what is essentially an entry-level marketing job?**

How to **answer** *it: During my many years at the agency, I have acquired many valuable skills. At the same time, I feel as if I've stopped growing. There's only so far you can go in such a career, and I am nearing the end of the career path. I am no longer challenged by my work, and being challenged is what keeps me motivated. I've thought about this for a long time, as switching careers is not an easy decision to make. Still, I am confident that I am doing the right thing by looking for a job within another industry, even if it means starting over.*

My interest in marketing arose last year when a local family lost their home to a fire. A group of people from my community decided to pitch in and help this family raise enough money to rebuild their home. I helped by designing and distributing posters, placing advertisements in local newspapers, and selling T-shirts outside grocery stores and shopping malls. When I began to see the result of what my work was doing, I became very excited about this task. I learned that you can have a great product and a great cause but that if nobody knows about it, you are dead in the water. I felt as if the work I was doing was making a difference, and I was good at it, too.

Since then, I have taken two introductory marketing courses and am planning to enroll in a part-time degree program this fall. Also, I'll be able to use many of the skills I've acquired working at an employment agency to benefit me in a marketing career as well. After all, working in an employment agency is marketing—that is, marketing the agency to corporate clients and job seekers, and marketing the job seekers to corporate clients.

The interviewer wants to determine two things: the candidate's motivation for choosing a new career and the likelihood that the candidate will be comfortable in a position in which she will probably have less power and responsibility than in previous jobs. To dispel the interviewer's fears, discuss your reasons for switching careers and be sure to show that you have a solid understanding of the position and the industry in general. Many candidates expect to start their new careers in jobs comparable to the one they held previously. The truth is that most career changers must start in a lower, if not entry-level, position in their new companies to gain basic experience and knowledge in the field.

 According to your resume, you were a manager at Crane Computer Store from 1990 through 1995 and then assistant manager at a different branch of the store starting in 1995. Were you demoted?

*How to **answer** it: This wasn't a demotion. I was originally manager of the Paper Products Department. It was a very small section. When an opening came up for an assistant manager in the Home PC Department at another store, I jumped at the chance. It was a much better opportunity because it was a much larger department, and I knew I would have greater responsibilities.*

Although the candidate's job title would indicate that she had been demoted, she explains why this wasn't actually the case. She was willing to trade the "manager" title for a job with more responsibility. If she had been demoted, however, she would need to explain why.

 Your resume says that you are an administrative assistant, yet you're applying for a job that has much more responsibility. What makes you think you can handle it?

*How to **answer** it: Even though my job title is administrative assistant, I have many more responsibilities than that title
usually implies. I train all new support staff and supervise
junior clerks.*

This answer explains how this candidate's responsibilities differed
from what one might assume from her job title. She chooses to
discuss the aspects of her current job that are related to the job she
is interviewing for.

Q: Have you ever been fired?

*How to **answer** it: When I was in college, I was fired from a
summer internship. I was working for a software consulting
company, and midway through the summer a new president
was appointed because of some financial difficulties. As one of
his first orders of business, he requested the resignation of my
entire work group. I was unexpectedly swept out with everyone
else, though my work performance had never been criticized.*

If you've never been fired, this should be an easy question to
answer. If you have been fired, you'll need to be prepared to discuss the situation in detail and possibly answer a series of specific
follow-up questions. If the termination was the result of a situation beyond your control, such as corporate downsizing, most
interviewers will be understanding. If you were fired due to poor
performance or some other personal problem, you'll need to admit
your fault and convince the interviewer that you've corrected the
problem. Although this may be a difficult question to answer
(and one that makes you—ultimately—nervous about the overall
impression you will leave behind), you should be completely honest. If you aren't honest and the recruiter finds out as much from
your references, you will definitely not be offered the job; if you
have been made an offer or have already accepted one, it may be
revoked or you may be subject to an immediate dismissal.

Q: **Your resume states that you were fired from your last job. I admire your honesty, but can you explain why this happened?**

*How to **answer** it: A new manager came in. I liked him, and I thought we worked well together. But a month after he arrived, he fired me. I heard afterward that many of the people I'd worked with were fired also, and he'd filled the empty slots with people from his previous job.*

Understanding why you were fired is the first important step to take if you want an employer to hire you. Any employer would be nervous and, in fact, foolish to hire someone who doesn't have a clue as to why she was fired. Own up to your mistakes; you'll stand a better chance of being hired.

Q: **In checking your resume we found that you were fired—and for a serious offense. Can you explain what happened?**

*How to **answer** it: It happened about five years ago. I got in with the wrong crowd; they would go out for drinks every night, and I wound up joining them. They were a rowdy bunch, not the kind of friends I would have picked if I could, but they were my colleagues, and I didn't have the courage to refuse them. But one night we stayed too late at a club and drank too much, and a fight started. One woman got hurt, and they had to rush her to the hospital. I didn't have anything to do with it, but the cops took us all in. I spent the night in jail, got bailed out in the morning, and when I went into work later that day, I got a pink slip. It was a hard lesson for me, but it changed my life. Since then, I've had two jobs, and though I'm always friendly with all my colleagues, when I walk out the door at night I don't socialize with them. I head home.*

Both situations are difficult for a prospective employer to accept. However, when a job hunter admits her mistake and has changed her ways, she stands a much better chance than someone who refuses to admit she might have been responsible for a serious offense.

Q: Would you be able to work extended hours if the job needed you to?

*How to **answer** it:* I'm accustomed to working long hours during the week. I usually work until at least 6:30 because I get a lot done after the office closes at five. I can make arrangements to be available on weekends if necessary, though I do prefer to have at least twenty-four hours' notice.

Your response should match closely the position you are applying for and should reflect a realistic understanding of the work and time required. Ask about seasonality of your work if you're unsure, and show a willingness to work occasional extended hours. If you are completely unwilling to work any overtime, it's not likely that many companies will consider you a very valuable asset. Recent studies have shown that a large majority of Americans are working, on average, closer to fifty hours per week than to forty.

Q: What are your salary requirements?

*How to **answer** it:* If hired, I would expect to earn a salary that is comparable to the going rate for someone in my field, with my same skills, amount of experience, and expertise. However, the salary of the job is not my only consideration. The opportunity, as you have presented it, is much more important to me. I really believe that this job is exactly in line with what I hope to accomplish, and that is the most important thing to me. What kind of range do you have in mind?

Recruiters weed out people whose financial goals are unrealistic or not in line with what the position is offering. This question is a direct hit, and both the interviewer and the candidate know that. It forces you to respond—directly—to a question relating to a very touchy subject. On the one hand, you may cite a salary that is too low. As a result, you will seem uninformed or (even worse) desperate. On the other hand, if you throw out a salary amount that is too high, you may eliminate yourself from any further consideration. The best way to handle the salary question is to turn the question back on the recruiter. Mention that the salary isn't your primary consideration, and ask what the salary range for the position is. Next, ask the recruiter to consider how your qualifications compare to the average requirements for the position and go from there.

Q: What is your current salary?

*How to **answer** it: I currently earn an annual salary of $45,000 per year with comprehensive company paid benefits.*

If you're asked a question this direct, consider yourself lucky. Telling the recruiter how much money you make now is a heck of a lot easier than trying to negotiate a salary with absolutely no information to go on (as in the previous question). Be sure not to embellish your salary, as this information can be very easy for an employer to find out. More and more companies are starting to verify applicants' pay history, some even demanding to see W-2 forms from job seekers. If you get the job, a falsehood discovered even years later may be grounds for immediate dismissal. Don't leave yourself open to this kind of trouble.

Q: Would you be willing to relocate to another city?

*How to **answer** it: Though I would prefer to remain here, it's certainly a possibility I'd be willing to consider based on the scope of the opportunity.*

Just because you're asked this question does not mean that the interviewer wants to fly you off to the other side of the country for a job. You may, even in some first interviews, be asked questions that seem to elicit a tremendous commitment on your behalf, such as this one. Although such questions may be unfair during an initial job interview, you may well conclude that you have nothing to gain and everything to lose with a negative response. If you are asked such a question unexpectedly during an initial job interview, simply say something like "That's certainly a possibility" or "I'm willing to consider that." If and when the interviewer says something along the lines of "Well, we have nothing for you in our Anchorage office, but our outfit in Mobile would certainly benefit from someone with your experience!" then you can begin to panic.

If you do receive an offer, you can find out the specific work conditions as far as relocation goes and then decide whether you wish to accept the position. Remember, at the job-offer stage, you have the most negotiating power, and the employer may be willing to accommodate your needs. If that isn't the case, you explain that upon reflection, you've decided you can't relocate but you'd like to be considered for other positions that might open up in the future.

Q: **Does the frequent travel that is required for this job fit in with your lifestyle?**

*How to **answer** it: The frequent travel in this consulting position is no problem for either me or my family. I was recently married, but my wife is an airline flight attendant, so neither of us follows the typical routine.*

If you feel comfortable enough to divulge information about your family situation, now is the time to do so. The interviewer's main concern here is that the candidate may not be able to travel as much as the job requires. To alleviate this concern, emphasize your flexibility or explain why travel wouldn't be a problem. Remember to be honest. If you were unaware that the job required any sort of travel—and if it would most likely be a problem—say so.

Q: Sell me this stapler.

*How to **answer** it: This professional quality stapler is both functional and attractive. It will help you reduce clutter on your desk by enabling you to fasten pages together. Since papers relating to the same subject will now be attached, you'll be more efficient, and you will spend less time searching for papers. Finally, its sleek shape and black color are coordinated to match the rest of your office furniture.*

The interviewer is curious as to how quickly you can react to a situation. Do you have the ability to think on your feet? Do you know how to communicate effectively and succinctly? This is one question that you're likely to be asked if you're applying for a sales or marketing position in particular. If you want to get into either of those industries, be prepared to give a thirty-second sales pitch on the benefits and advantages of any common office staple, from a paper clip to a BlackBerry.

Q: Prove to me that your interest in this job and company is sincere.

*How to **answer** it: I know that many people would like to work in television because of large income potential or the opportunity to be on camera, but my reasons go far beyond that. To me, communication is an art form, and the television industry is the ultimate test of how well one communicates. Working in television isn't like working for a newspaper, where, if a reader misses a fact, he can just go back and reread it. A television news story can go by in a flash, and the challenge is to make sure the audience understands it, learns from it, and, in a broader sense, can use the information to* *better their lives or their situations. It's the way television can evoke action that's always made me want to be a part of the industry. I'm particularly interested in this station because I like your focus on the community. Though the on-air products have a great look, the station seems to remain focused on the tradition of local news and what matters to its audience. The special reports that emphasize town politics and explain the big issues facing a community make the viewer feel that the station is a part of the community. In my opinion, this is a great way to maintain a loyal audience.*

Being unprepared to answer this question can eliminate you from further consideration. On the other hand, if you are able to demonstrate a strong interest in the company and the position, you'll have an advantage over the competition. Be sure to talk about the specific position and give the details of the company that make you want to become an employee.

Let's say you are faced with this statement: "You have seven minutes to convince me you're the best candidate for the job. Go." How would you react? The question is essentially the question that can determine whether you're paying attention to the material in this book. This is the question that only the most prepared of all job interviewees will survive, and that's exactly what the recruiter is looking for. In answering this question, you should refer back to everything this book has taught you. Review your personal themes and touch upon each and every one of them. Assure the interviewer that you know all there is to know about the job, the company, and the industry. Essentially, you are trying to be every recruiter's dream candidate. It's not an easy thing to pull off, but have faith, you can do it. You can win that job!

Q: You've been working outside the banking industry for the past year. Can you explain why you want to return now?

How to **answer** *it: Yes, I can. The job market, as you know, has been bad for the past year and a half. It's been impossible for someone with my qualifications to find a job in the banking industry. To support my family, I had to take jobs in retail sales. I was happy to see your ad for a banking job that needs someone with my skills in branch management.*

This candidate's only choice is to be honest. He is not to blame for the bad job market, so he makes no excuses for working outside his field for a year.

 Your resume states that when you got caught up in the burst of the tech bubble you decided not to look for a job but to freelance as a consultant. How did that work out for you, and why are you back in the job market?

How to **answer** *it: I enjoyed consulting. It worked out well for almost two years. But I found it hard to do everything—to keep looking for clients and at the same time service the ones I had. I also missed the collegial atmosphere of working with a team. I'm eager to return to that atmosphere. I don't regret the two years I spent consulting, however. I learned a lot during those years, and I'm bringing with me the valuable lessons I learned.*

No one likes to feel second-best. Why should an employer hire anyone who isn't fully committed to the company and his job? Most employers, however, would be intrigued by a prospective employee who is bringing new skills and ideas to the job.

 I see from your resume you were laid off from your job six months ago. Why haven't you taken another job?

How to **answer** *it: I decided I needed to brush up on some skills that might have prevented my being laid off. Also, I thought these skills would help me in my job search and, ultimately, prove an asset in my career.*

Six months is a long hiatus between jobs. Your prospective employer is right to be curious about what you were doing during that time. He's not interested in the time you spent on the beach. He wants to know what skills you learned that might help him in his business. Also, he might see behind that Mexican trip and decide that you're having trouble finding a new job. If so, this makes one more reason you won't be hired.

Q: **Your resume indicates that you have not worked for several years. Would you mind explaining this absence?**

*How to **answer** it:* I have spent the past five years raising my son, Liam, who's now in kindergarten. Leaving the workplace was a very difficult decision for me, but as this was our first child, I didn't think I would be able to commit to my career 100 percent, knowing the responsibilities I had at home. Since I didn't think it would be fair to my employer to give any less than 100 percent, I believe it was the right decision for me at the time. Now that my son is old enough to be in school, I feel refreshed and am completely ready to devote myself to a full-time career.

Whatever the reason for your hiatus, be honest. The interviewer has the right to know why you have not worked in so long, as it could relate to the job you are being considered for. Discuss the decisions behind your absence, whether they were to stay at home and raise a family or recuperate from a debilitating injury. Be sure to emphasize the reasons why you want to return to work and why you think you are ready. Most importantly, stress your eagerness to resume your career.

Q: **What made you decide that you were now ready to pursue full-time employment again?**

*How to **answer** it:* I took a leave of absence to care for my elderly father. This was prior to our family making *arrangements for his transfer to an adult home. It took some time to find the appropriate residence and get him settled in comfortably, but now I am confident he is getting good care and that I can focus on work and not be distracted by personal issues.*

While you don't have to defend your absence, your response should make good sense to the interviewer so that you can dispel any fear of an inability to commit to the job at hand. Sometimes candidates are uncomfortable giving up too much information about their personal lives, but providing a few sentences on this absence justifies the time frame and offers a "that was then, this is now" validation.

Q: Have you kept current with what is going on in the field?

How to **answer** *it: Absolutely. Even though I have been out of the industry for several years, I continue to read all the trade journals and subscribe to current Internet newsletters on emerging trends and new case studies. I'm very eager to put some of these ideas into practice now and can see how they would be very applicable to your company's growth mission. I've also maintained my membership status in the professional association for my skill area, so I still have networking access as well.*

Employers want to know you have something to contribute from day one. A returnee who needs time to get up to speed will not appear as desirable as one who has done her homework. Additionally, if your time off has been of a significant length, you need to project flexibility. Nothing scares an employer more than thinking you might be stuck in old ways of doing things or have difficulty adapting to new processes.

I see you were manager at Wanda's Whispers. What type of business is that and what did you do there?

How to **answer** *it: Wanda's Whispers is a retail store that sells women's lingerie. I was the store manager. I interviewed, hired, and trained the store's sales team.*

Although the candidate may be embarrassed to discuss the nature of the business, she proudly discusses her responsibilities there.

 I see you have a GED. Why did you drop out of high school?

How to **answer** *it: I guess I was young and foolish then. It was a long time ago. I thought I didn't need school anymore, but I was sadly mistaken. I got my GED three years later and then went on to college. I'm looking forward to applying my training as a registered nurse to this position.*

Youthful indiscretions can be forgiven. Although this candidate dropped out of high school, he did continue his education and is planning to move forward with his career.

 Why are you applying for a job outside your major?

How to **answer** *it: I know I can use the skills I developed as a psychology major to succeed in marketing research. I have taken courses in consumer behavior, statistics, and research design, which I know will be useful in this field.*

This candidate shows how her skills are transferable to this field. She makes no mention of what her future plans are for staying in this field or going back to psychology.

 You didn't start working until two years after you got your degree. What were you doing?

*How to **answer** it: I traveled extensively the year after I graduated from college. I backpacked across Europe for three months, and then I spent four months in Australia. After that, I traveled throughout the United States.*

Had this candidate said that she sat at home watching television for a year after graduating, the interviewer would have assumed she was a little low on motivation. However, she explored the world, which was an admirable use of her time and broadened her experience.

Q: **Your resume doesn't show any formal training in this field. What do you think qualifies you for this job?**

*How to **answer** it: While I don't have formal training in this field, I do have a lot of practical experience. As you can see from my resume, on my last job I spent a tremendous amount of time doing research. I plan to begin taking some courses so I can get my degree in this field.*

This interviewee explains how her experience has given her the skills she needs to do this job. She also talks about her intention to get some formal training.

Q: **You're so young. What makes you think you can do a good job?**

*How to **answer** it: I have a lot of experience in retail. I started working as a retail clerk straight out of high school, and over the past three years I worked my way up to assistant manager.*

Rather than letting the interviewer lead her into a discussion about her age, this candidate leads him into a discussion about her experience.

Illegal Questions

 How old are you?

*How to **answer** it: I prefer to think of myself in terms of experience and not age. I have worked in this industry for quite some time. I have seen it go from a small playing field to what it is today. Fortunately I have kept up with all the changes by taking classes and constantly updating my skills.*

Rather than address the issue of age, or the inappropriateness of this question, this candidate has instead decided to address some positive things about himself. He has a lot of experience, and he strives to keep himself abreast of changes in the industry by taking classes.

 How much do you weigh?

*How to **answer** it: My weight isn't an issue. I have never had a problem performing my job duties.*

This question is not only rude, it may be illegal as well. This candidate explains how her weight doesn't affect her ability to do her job.

 What is your race?

*How to **answer** it: I'm African American and Asian.*

If an employer asks a question about race, his intentions are usually not good, so make a mental note that you were asked. If the employer discriminates against you based on your race, the information you provided in this answer can be used as evidence against him if you file a complaint with the Equal Employment Opportunity Commission.

Were you born in the United States?

*How to **answer** it: I'm not sure why you're asking me that. Can you explain?*

This question is inappropriate, and the employer probably knows that. The candidate gives him a chance to correct himself. Perhaps all the employer needs to know is that the candidate is eligible to work in the United States.

Where were your parents born?

*How to **answer** it: My parents came to this country thirty years ago. They worked very hard to put me through school and are very proud of my successful career. They passed their work ethic down to me.*

This candidate chooses not to reveal his national origin and instead manages to talk about his own qualities. There is nothing that says a candidate shouldn't reveal his national origin, just that he doesn't have to.

Q: Your last name sounds Spanish. Is it?

*How to **answer** it: Yes, it is.*

The applicant has a choice to make. She can refuse to answer, or she can just give a simple answer. If this was the only question of this type, the interviewer may have just been trying to make conversation.

Q: What is your sexual orientation?

*How to **answer** it: I don't think that has anything to do with this job.*

Sexual orientation isn't something that should be discussed on a job interview.

What is your religious background?

*How to **answer** it: I consider religion a very personal thing, so I would rather not discuss it.*

The applicant can always choose to politely refuse to answer a question she considers improper. That is what she decides to do.

 Do you have any children?

*How to **answer** it: I understand that you may be concerned that having a family might get in the way of someone's career. However, that has never been the case with me. I'm very dedicated to my career.*

Without giving a direct answer to this question, the candidate has chosen to reassure the employer that having a family, or not having one, will not influence her career.

 Are you planning to have children?

*How to **answer** it: I am very committed to my career. Whether or not I have children will not affect that.*

This interviewee tells the employer the only thing he has the right to know—that she is dedicated to her career.

Q: **Are you married?**

*How to **answer** it: No, I'm not.*

Although this question is inappropriate and may be illegal, depending on where you live, the candidate sees no harm in answering it.

 **Do you belong to a union?**

*How to **answer** it: Will I be required to join a union?*

The National Labor Relations Act prohibits employers from questioning applicants about their union sympathies. This candidate chooses to avoid the question by asking her own.

Are you a Democrat or Republican?

How to answer it: I've always felt that it's a bad idea to discuss religion or politics with anyone. Therefore, I'm going to refrain from answering that question.

The candidate has given a polite answer, but has refused to provide the information the interviewer improperly requested.

Will your religion keep you from working on Saturday or Sunday?

How to answer it: Perhaps we can discuss the details of my schedule after we both confirm that I'm the right candidate for this position.

This candidate knows Title VII of the Civil Rights Act requires that an employer reasonably accommodate the religious practices of an employee or applicant as long as doing so doesn't pose a hardship. He also knows that an employer cannot decide to reject a candidate based on the knowledge that this accommodation will be necessary. However, he chooses to wait until he receives an offer before discussing this.

Have you ever been arrested or convicted of a crime?

How to answer it: No. I have never been convicted of a crime.

An employer may not ask you if you have ever been arrested, but you can be legally asked if you've been convicted of a crime. Notice how this candidate avoids the arrest question. She doesn't want to lie or discuss an arrest that she was not convicted for.

Have you ever committed a crime?

*How to **answer** it: If you're asking if I've ever been convicted of a crime, no, I haven't.*

An employer may ask if an applicant has been convicted of a crime, but he may not ask if he has committed one or if he has been arrested.

 I see you're limping. Did you hurt yourself?

*How to **answer** it: I'm fine, thank you.*

The employer, according to the Americans with Disabilities Act, cannot inquire about an applicant's injury, and the candidate is under no obligation to reveal it.

 Do you have a heart condition?

*How to **answer** it: With all due respect, I don't have to answer that question.*

The applicant has a right to refuse to answer this question. The ADA makes questions about one's health illegal.

Will you need us to make any accommodations for you to do your job?

*How to **answer** it: I am able to perform all functions of the job as you described it.*

ADA prohibits the employer from asking this question, even if she asks it of all applicants. The only reason an employer may ask this question is if the applicant's disability is obvious and the employer has good reason to believe she will need accommodation.

Have you ever been treated for mental health problems?

*How to **answer** it:* I have, but everything is under control now. I have always performed well at work, and I know I will continue to do so.

Although the candidate is under no obligation to reveal this information at any time, he knows he may need reasonable accommodation in the future.

 Have you ever been treated for drug addiction?

*How to **answer** it:* That was some time ago, and I prefer not to discuss it.

This candidate is within her rights not to discuss this. People who have been treated for drug addiction are covered by the ADA, and a hiring decision cannot be based upon this.

 Travel is a big part of this job. Will your family be okay with that?

*How to **answer** it:* I can assure you that traveling will not be a problem. I traveled extensively on my previous job.

This candidate has chosen to let the employer know that her family status will not affect her job. She mentions the fact that her previous job had similar requirements, and it wasn't a problem.

 You're a young single guy living in the city. How do you handle having women chase after you?

*How to **answer** it:* Work has always been my priority.

It is inappropriate for the employer to ask a question regarding the applicant's sex life. The candidate chooses to evade the question by talking about work.

KEY WORDS (AND) PHRASES

Analyze

Recommend

In hindsight

Consistent with results

Come up with a revised plan

Real benefits

More sizzle

Take care of all the details

Excellent proofreader

Accept responsibility

Don't make excuses

Improve on my past mistakes

Prevent a problem

Vigilant

Encouraging

Cross each bridge when I come to it

Take it all in stride

Alternate plans

Changing plans

Additional training

Stickler for detail

Feedback

Extensive background

I'm committed to working in this field.

I know I can do a good job here.

I'm interested in your organization.

Make a difference

Better opportunity

Greater responsibilities

I'm accustomed to working long hours.

Salary that's comparable to the going rate
Salary is not my only consideration.
Scope of opportunity
Collegial atmosphere
Brush up on my skills
Not distracted by personal issues
Membership status in professional organizations
I have taken courses.

Chapter 9

Asking Your Own Questions

As the interview nears its end, you will be given a chance to ask questions of your own. It is imperative that you are ready for that opportunity when it comes. Your questions will show the interviewer that you are interested in the job. The fact that you take time to ask questions will also show her that you are a careful decision-maker who needs to gather information before making a decision that is as serious as accepting a job offer. Your questions also show that you were paying attention during the interview.

You should prepare several questions before the job interview. Think of what information will help you decide whether you want to work for this employer. You will want to know about the company's future plans for growth, its current financial health, rates of employee turnover, levels of job satisfaction among employees, and what your chances for advancement are.

You may very likely come up with more questions during the interview. Don't be afraid to ask for clarification of anything you didn't understand. Questions about salary, benefits, and vacation time are off limits at this point. Hold on to those until an official job offer has been made.

Why the Job Is Open

Q: **Why is this job open?**

This information will help you understand how you will be received should a job offer be made to you and should you accept it. If the person you will be replacing has left under difficult circumstances, that is, if he was fired or was otherwise forced to leave, his former coworkers may be resentful of anyone who fills his place. If the previous employee was promoted within the company, you taking the job may give you a chance for similar advancement down the line.

Q: **How many people have held this position in the past three years? Why did they leave?**

If there is a high rate of turnover in the position you are interviewing for, you should be suspicious. You should try to find out why this is the case. Is this a difficult employer to work for? Or perhaps the company has expectations that are impossible for employees to meet, and they are fired for not meeting them. If you haven't already, access your network to find out if anyone has had any experience with this employer.

Q: **How will you decide who to hire?**

The answer to this question will let you find out if you missed something during the interview. Was there another skill or qualification the employer is seeking that you didn't get to talk about? By the time you get to ask this question, the interview will be drawing to a close. However, you can still follow up by sending a thank-you letter that will highlight the particular qualifications that you have and the employer is seeking.

Q: **When will you make a decision?**

If you know when the employer will make a hiring decision, you won't be left in a state of limbo waiting for the phone to ring. You can call the employer yourself, but it's best to wait one day after the employer says the decision is going to be made. If you are continuing to interview for other jobs, which you should do until you receive and accept a job offer, you might decide to schedule future interviews after that date, if it is close.

Job Responsibilities

Q: Is there a written job description? May I see it?

You will ask this question simply because you need this information to make an informed decision about whether or not to accept the job.

Q: You mentioned something about a training period. How long is it?

This question indicates your interest in the job and shows that you were listening during the interview. It allows you to get clarification.

Q: Are there any other opportunities for training?

An employee who inquires about training opportunities is willing to learn as much as possible to do a good job.

Q: What types of assignments will I have?

This question indicates that you are interested in the job. It also allows you to learn what you will be doing if you are hired.

Q: What improvements do you want to make here and how can I help you make them?

You will phrase this question the same way you phrased the previous one, allowing the employer to envision you as the person he will hire. It will give you a glimpse into the job and the company's plans for the future.

Opportunities for Advancement

Q: **What does one need to do to advance?**

Asking this question shows that you will be a productive employee who is interested in doing the best job possible. You will do what you need to do to move up.

Q: **What are the chances for advancement?**

Similar in nature to the previous question, this question shows the employer that you are motivated. It also allows you to find out if you will have the opportunity to advance should you work for that employer. That information will help you decide whether to accept a job offer, since you don't want to languish in the same position for a long time.

Q: **How often are performance evaluations conducted and how are the evaluations made?**

You will ask this question to learn what working for this company will be like. You may get a sense of how strict the managers are or how closely the staff is monitored. If you are interviewing for a management position, you will get a sense of how much of your time you will spend on evaluation paperwork.

Who Your Supervisor Is

Q: **What is the chain of command?**

Whenever you ask questions about the inner workings of the company, it indicates to the employer that you are interested in the job.

Q: **Who will I be reporting to?**

If you find out who your immediate supervisor is, you can try to learn about that person. Don't forget that you should be gathering information that will help you decide whether to accept an offer if one is made.

Company History and Growth

Q: How long have you worked here?

The person interviewing you is in a job that is probably several steps above the one that you are interviewing for. Given that fact, the answer to this question will indicate how employees typically advance within the company. If the owner of the company is interviewing you, there is no reason to ask this question.

Q: What do you like most about your job with this company?

The interviewer is likely one of the few employees of the company with whom you will have contact before making your decision. See what she has to say about working there. The answer to this question, if the interviewer is honest, will weigh in to your decision about accepting a job offer. As with the previous question, ask this only of employees and not the owner of the company.

Q: How long do most employees stay?

Learning about turnover is a good way to gauge whether employees enjoy working for the employer. A high rate of turnover indicates that most employees aren't satisfied with their jobs, while a low rate of turnover demonstrates a high level of job satisfaction.

Q: What reason do most employees give for leaving?

The answer to this question expands on the answer to the prior question. Knowing why employees leave the company helps you find out what you may or may not like about working there. Of course, the interviewer may not know the answer to this question or may not be willing to share it.

Q: **How has the company grown over the past five years? Is it profitable?**

A company's financial health will help you decide whether to accept a job offer. If the company hasn't grown over the past five years or if it isn't profitable, this should signal that it might not be in the best financial health. Should you accept a job offer, you may be looking for work again soon.

Q: **What does the company plan to do to keep growing and what role would I play?**

The answer to this question will give you information about your prospective employer and the job. You will learn what expectations the employer has for you. By phrasing the question like this, you give the interviewer the chance to picture you in the job he is interviewing you for.

Q: **In your opinion, how does this company compare to its major competitors, like Activate, Pump, and Dragon Works?**

In preparing for the interview, you should have researched the prospective employer. When you ask this question, you are saying to the interviewer, "Look at the research I've done. I know who your competitors are." The answer to this question will also help you learn more about the company.

Q: **From my research, I learned you sell your products both in the United States and Canada. Do you plan to expand into any other markets?**

Again you are stating something you uncovered in your research. You are also trying to learn something further about the company.

Q: I know you sell hair-care products. What are the demographics of your customers?

Your reason for asking this question is similar to your reason for asking the prior one. If you have experience with the demographic this company targets, that is something you can talk about in your thank-you letter or in any follow-up interviews.

Q: You mentioned that several of your clients are in the apparel business. What industries are your other clients in?

This question shows you were paying attention during the interview. You also want to learn more about the company's other clients, which demonstrates your interest in the company.

Questions Not to Ask

Avoid asking the interviewer the following questions.

Q: Never ask: How much money will I make?

Money should never be discussed on a job interview. You should hold off on discussing salary until you receive a job offer, when you will be able to negotiate. Even if the employer brings it up first, it is best to avoid getting into an extensive conversation about it at this point.

Q: Never ask: What are the health benefits like?

While you may need this information to help you decide whether or not to accept a job offer, the interview isn't the time to obtain it. Hold off on this discussion until you receive a job offer. The person interviewing you may not even know a lot about company benefits other than those he has.

Q: Never ask: **How much vacation time will I have?**

You haven't even started working and already you want to know about time off. Your goal during the interview is to demonstrate to the employer that you will be a productive employee. Asking about vacation time will not help you reach that goal.

Q: Never ask: **Can I take time off for religious observance?**

An employer is required by law to give you time off for religious observance, so you have no reason to ask about it during the interview. It should never be brought up in the interview or usually anytime before you begin working.

Q: Never ask: **What does it take to get fired?**

Asking this question is kind of like saying, "I want to do as little as possible to get by." Is that how you want the employer to see you?

Chapter 10

Industry-
Specific **Buzz
Words** and
Phrases

EVERY INDUSTRY HAS ITS OWN VOCABULARY THAT DESCRIBES THE JOB RESPONSIBILITIES of its workers. These Key Words and Phrases are known as buzz words. Using buzz words to talk about your experience and interest in a job can make you stand out because it shows that you speak the same language as the interviewer. This chapter contains a list of fifteen common industries and some well-known buzz words associated with their professions. Each section also lists examples of phrases you can use when answering questions about your work experience.

Accounting and Finance

Accounting and finance buzz words highlight experience with accounting, budgeting, treasury, auditing, and information systems activities. This includes collection, documentation, and analysis of financial data and the use of this data to make strategic decisions and share pertinent information with investors, regulators, and government entities. It also includes allocation of capital required for annual operations as well as growth.

▶ Buzz Words

Accounting
Analytical services
Asset management
Audits
Bonds
Brokerage services
Budgeting
Capital
Client relations
Commodities
Consumer Confidence Index (CCI)
Corporate and municipal securities
Credit analysis
Derivatives
Financial analysis
Foreign markets
Global markets
Home loans
Insurance products
International banking services
IRS filing
Lending
Management services
Managerial accounting
Mergers and acquisitions
Online investments
Payroll
Private client services
Real estate and mortgage loans
Retail banking
SEC reporting
Securities services
Tax filings

Transaction management
Trust and banking markets
Underwriting

▶ **Phrases to Use When Describing Your Skills and Experience**

- Managed all aspects of finance, accounting, foreign exchange dealings, marketing, and data processing of company and its overseas offices.
- Reviewed finances and securities pertaining to advances and shipping for client of about 200.
- Audited private companies; listed companies, partnerships, and individual business.
- Prepared financial statements and schedules.
- Settled bond and equity transactions in the United States markets.
- Generated income statements, balance sheets, general ledger, checks, and reports.
- Entered payable vouchers.
- Performed all accounting functions to include journal entries, accounts payable and receivable, petty cash, deposits, bank reconciliations, and trial balance.
- Controlled budget, cash flow, and capital expenditures.
- Developed corporate and project-oriented financial strategies.

Administrative

These buzz words are for applicants looking for general management and office positions. They reflect an involvement and familiarity with general office management as well as oversight of facilities and systems associated with the day-to-day organizational activities. Important skills include administrative, project management, customer service, and light labor.

▶ Buzz Words

Administrative support services
Association membership
Business administration
Client relations
Customer service
Data entry
Database management
Event planning
File maintenance
Information trafficking
Invoicing
Mass mailings
Meeting planning
Meetings
Office management and operations
Organization policies and procedures
Procedural enhancement
Public relations
Reconciliation
Report generation
Sales support
Supervisory skills
Travel arrangements
Troubleshooting
Vendor relations
Word processing

▶ Phrases to Use When Describing Your Skills and Experience

- Translated survey data into numerical code for data entry.
- Designed forms for archive.
- Assisted in revising physical inventory procedures.
- Served as principal consultant on plant inventory systems.

- Developed nationwide relocation policy and procedures for new employees.
- Provided word processing, customer relations, and some accounts payable processing.
- Handled incoming calls; scheduled appointments.
- Supervised employees to ensure observation of rules/regulations.
- Provided customer service; resolved complaints.
- Coordinated catering for special events.
- Budgeted and facilitated four-day professional seminar.
- Secured new business using customer inquiries and mass mailing responses.
- Scheduled site visits and installations.
- Collected, sorted, and distributed incoming mail.
- Created effective product displays.
- Monitored equipment and supply inventories.
- Performed analysis of client files.

Biotechnological and Pharmaceuticals

The buzz words in these industries are often highly technical, and they exhibit a science background with in-depth familiarity of biology and chemistry. Resumes may demonstrate experience with cell biology, vaccine research, prescription drugs, over-the-counter medicines, chemical compounds used in pharmaceuticals, and tools used to diagnose diseases. Relevant experience includes synthesizing new drugs, testing of drugs, determination of dosages and delivery forms (such as liquid or tablets), calculating cost-effectiveness of a proposed drug, and selling/marketing of pharmaceuticals.

▶ **Buzz Words**
Advanced cellular and molecular biology
Agricultural biotechnology

Biomedical research

Biostatistics

Chemical manufacturing

Clinical trials

Critical care products

Development and consulting

Diagnostic tests

Drug optimization programs

Epidemiological research

FDA compliance strategies

Genetics

Health care policy

Immunology

Infectious diseases

Metabolic diseases

Patient care

Pharmaceuticals

Public health research

Reproductive disorders

Tissue and organ replacement

Urology/gynecology studies

Veterinary applications

▶ **Phrases to Use When Describing Your Skills and Experience**
- Contributed to the discovery and preclinical development of antiviral compounds.
- Designed and implemented in vitro and in vivo drug metabolism and pharmacokinetic experiments to facilitate the selection and optimization of drug candidates.
- Identified potential metabolites by using state-of-the-art technologies from in vitro and in vivo studies.
- Performed tasks that support study conduct, according to all applicable regulations and operations procedures.

- Used and maintained standard Medical Affairs tracking tools.
- Performed initial review of regulatory and required study documents.
- Responsible for inventory management of nonclinical supply materials.
- Applied knowledge of therapeutic area and drug development (investigational, observational, surveillance).
- Trained others on job-related functions.

Communications

Industry buzz words in the area of communications highlight writing, graphics, public relations, publicity, and promotions skills and experience. This includes activities associated with creating, distributing, and transmitting text and graphic information via varied print, video, audio, computer, and web-based media.

▶ **Buzz Words**
Acquisition of titles
Book production
Casting contracts
Communications management
Content development
Data management
Desktop publishing
Editorial direction
Fact checking
Health care communications systems
Layout
Marketing proposals
Media relations
Periodical publishing
Publishing process
Standards and procedures

Story development
Trade magazines
Trade newspaper
Work flow systems
Writing

▶ **Phrases to Use When Describing Your Skills and Experience**

- Proofread archaeological monographs and museum catalogues.
- Edited and typed grant proposals, research papers, and reports.
- Researched and wrote items for annual fact books and their weekly supplemental updates covering the communications industry.
- Reported and wrote articles and columns for twice-monthly newspaper for the arts and entertainment industry.
- Supervised the design and production of titles for two continuity programs.
- Acted as liaison for Marketing Director, Editor, and advertisers.
- Edited three medical textbooks.
- Wrote campaign letters; ordered all campaign materials; staffed Campaign Advisory Committee; coordinated and directed chapter-wide meetings; conducted staff meetings.
- Drafted press releases and speeches.
- Researched and generated story ideas.
- Assisted in the production of industrial films, business presentations, videotaping of plays, fashion shows, and more.

Computers and Mathematics

For positions in the computer industry, buzz words are highly technical and change fairly rapidly. Effective buzz words highlight experience with defining, analyzing, and resolving business problems and using knowledge of computer systems to examine problems and design solutions. *Important skills and experience include planning new computer systems or devising ways to apply existing systems to operations that are still done manually.* Resumes for positions in mathematics should spotlight activities ranging from the creation of new theories and techniques to the translation of economic, scientific, engineering, and managerial problems into mathematical terms.

▶ **Buzz Words**

Algorithms

Backup and multiplatform connectivity systems

C++

CMS-2

COBOL programming

Computer systems

Data acquisition

Database management

Database repair/troubleshooting

Developmental math

DOD telecommunications technology, architecture, policy, and standards

Drivers

Information architecture

IT planning

LAN management

MIS

Network configuration

Networking solutions

Operating efficiencies

Preproduction testing

Real-time computer programs

Software development
Software testing
System design engineering
Systems test and integration
Technology integration
Video communications
Workstation maintenance

▶ Phrases to Use When Describing Your Skills and Experience

- Designed network-based applications for manufacturing process control and test data collection, improving product quality and manufacturing efficiency.
- Designed and maintained computer-based electronic test hardware.
- Developed online message system for members of the programming group.
- Supported existing clients and resolved critical issues/ problems in a timely fashion.
- Maintained and supported the existing COBOL mainframe online and batch systems.
- Researched and identified modern replacement hardware architecture for existing real-time simulation.
- Researched, identified, and developed a high-speed data communication system connecting an Intel Hypercube and Sun Sparc Workstation.
- Managed large data migration effort.
- Assisted sales force in technical presentations for prospective clients.
- Reduced process time and purchasing errors by developing an online program, allowing the purchasing department to track the status of all invoices.

Engineering

Buzz words from the various fields of engineering demonstrate experience with the theories and principles of science and mathematics and with designing machinery, products, systems, and processes for efficient and economical performance. This includes designing industrial machinery and equipment for manufacturing goods, defense systems, and weapons for the armed forces. Other important skills and experience include planning and supervising the construction of buildings, highways, and rapid transit systems and also designing and developing consumer products and systems for control and automation of manufacturing, business, and management processes.

▶ **Buzz Words**

3D modeling
Assembly design
C programming
C4 navigation and intelligence
Complex electromechanical systems
Conceptualization
Data collection and analysis
Design methodologies
Electrical design
Engineering management
Facilities engineering
Geological formations
High-temperature environments
Injection molding design
Manufacturing
Mechanical and control systems
Performance characteristics
Process and procedure development
Professional consulting

Research and development (R&D)
Structural design
Test planning and field operations
Top-level system architecture
Vendor and partner technology relationships

▶ **Phrases to Use When Describing Your Skills and Experience**
- Applied knowledge of thermodynamics, reactor design, phase separation, fluid compression and expansion, and process control to complete simulation from preliminary coding.
- Provided structural design and engineering estimates, and specifications for industrial, laboratory, commercial, and power facilities.
- Evaluated new computer product designs, solving environmental problems on prototype computers.
- Assisted engineers working on load monitors, which gauge weight and distribution properties on heavy machine presses.
- Conducted a variety of tests including Tensile, Compression, and Creep tests on modeled parts.
- Assembled machines from drawing specifications, wire electrical boards, test and trace defects.
- Observed and participated in exploration of mines surrounding Great Salt Lake.
- Repaired generators, electrical motors, and mechanical systems in shop, yard, and aboard rail units for public transport.

Executive and Managerial

Executive and managerial positions exist in all types of businesses. "Administrative" on page 192 contains a number of words that are also relevant to applicants seeking to be managers in an office setting. Executive buzz words should highlight experience ranging from general supervisory duties to running an entire company. Relevant skills include management of individual departments within a larger corporate structure, motivating workers to achieve their goals as rapidly and economically as possible, budgeting and directing projects, and evaluating company processes and methods to determine cost-effective plans.

▶ **Buzz Words**

Account management

Asset management

Benefits coordination

Branch management

Budget development

Business development

Client relations

Contract management

Customer service

Franchise management

Lead development

Major accounts

New business development

Product awareness

Provider/client communication

Relationship management

Revenue development

Sales objectives

Team management

Troubleshooting

Yearly transactions

▶ **Phrases to Use When Describing Your Skills and Experience**

- Obtained new accounts to replace lost business and maintain profitability.

- Used sales expertise and account management to develop 80 percent-new client base and maintain profit margins.
- Administered and directed marketing activities of banking operations.
- Organized and planned actions impacting on various sectors of bank's markets.
- Worked with other internal divisions and outside agencies to develop plans that supported division's activities.
- Planned and supervised training activities.
- Organized a smoothly functioning administration and operational division.
- Maintained detailed knowledge of all aspects to include maintenance, logistics, and communications.
- Trained and supervised three claims adjusters.

Government

For people interested in positions in politics and government, buzz words highlight experience in executive, legislative, judicial, or general government agencies as well as with public agencies, such as firefighting, military, police work, or the United States Postal Service. This includes researching and evaluating military materials; cleaning, maintenance, and general service for public works; participating in political campaigns by networking, fundraising, or organizing; and working to control narcotic and dangerous drug use through prevention and law enforcement. It also includes mail pickup and delivery experience, public relations and press work, and public outreach activities.

▶ **Buzz Words**

Administrative services
Agency management
Briefing reports
Central management agencies

Consumer rights

Defense contract management

Department of Labor and Workforce Development

Economic and educational support

Environmental studies

Field offices

Foreign intelligence

Governmental organization

Human health protection

Information services

Issuance of licenses

Local government agency

Maintenance and improvement

Medicaid services

Metropolitan development

National health programs

Nonprofit

Organization analysis

Political and legislative support functions

Productivity of natural resources

Public works

Recycling services

Regulatory commission

Security products

State government

Transportation planning

U.S. policy

Urban development

Work force conditions

▶ **Phrases to Use When Describing Your Skills and Experience**

- Demonstrated problem-solving skills and diplomatic capabilities in dealing with federal labor-management relations.

- Campaigned for the Democratic Party, focusing on significant economic changes, recycling services, regulation of companies, and safe living conditions.
- Processed incoming and outgoing mail for sorting and distribution; updated postal rates and sold stamps.
- Managed fire prevention activities and the protection of citizens in fire or medical emergencies.
- Dispatched law enforcement officers and rescue personnel in emergency situations.
- Supervised daily functions at national park, including trash pickup, water supply, and repair services; managed park headquarters.
- Volunteered at center for senior services and welfare. Responsibilities included helping to ensure safe living conditions, tracking Medicaid services, and being on call for emergency situations.
- Investigated cases of worker's compensation claims for public defender and compiled statistical material into spreadsheets.
- Raised drug prevention awareness by organizing support functions and seminars.
- Practiced law as a public defender in district court for ten years, primarily handling cases concerning domestic disputes and custody battles.

Health and Medical

Buzz words from the vital health and medical fields demonstrate experience with illness, working toward achieving and maintaining healthy lifestyles, and helping to address and resolve related issues, such as insurance and medical claim forms. This includes working directly with patients and their families in dealing with health problems; assisting patients by providing medical advice regarding prescriptions, insurance claim forms, and related issues; and researching medical treatments and techniques.

► **Buzz Words**

Ambulatory services
Appointments
Behavioral programs
Budget responsibilities
Business management activities
Case management
Clerical support
Clinical instruction
Comprehensive care
Crisis intervention
DEA regulations
Discharge planning
Disease research
Educational counseling
Emergency care
Formal education programs
Hematology and serology testing
Human services
In-patient and outpatient care
Laboratory operations
Medical management
Multidisciplined practice
Nursing services
Patient services
Pediatric/emergency medicine
Pharmacology and behavioral modification methods
Policy and procedures development
Private practice
Psychiatric care
Referring physicians

Respiratory therapy
Social services
Surgical procedures
Therapy
Ultrasound
X-ray department

▶ **Phrases to Use When Describing Your Skills and Experience**

- Provided spinal manipulation and handled necessary muscular-skeletal needs of sports-injured patients.
- Provided information for insurance companies, workman's compensation, and third-party billing procedures.
- Supervised seventy-five clinical, administrative, and staff employees.
- Coordinated treatment and discharge planning.
- Prepared patients for surgical procedures, recorded temperature and blood pressure, inserted intravenous units, and administered sedatives.
- Scheduled patients for appointments.
- Monitored radiographs and administered Novocain prior to procedures.
- Assisted dentist in prophylactic procedures: provided necessary tools, sterilized equipment, and comforted patients.
- Taught intensive aerobics, calisthenics, and stretching to co-educational classes of up to twenty-five adults in all physical conditions.
- Organized labs for veterinary students and for clinical instruction.
- Directed hygienic procedures on 300 animals, including surgical and necropsies.
- Instructed and supervised home health aides.

- Served as clinical instructor for physical therapy students and pulmonary clinic.
- Drafted physical therapy standards of care for selected surgical procedures.
- Requisitioned all laboratory supplies; participated in conferences with medical staff on patients with special laboratory needs.
- Conducted hematology and serology testing, as well as test sample photography.
- Operated hematology laboratory, using haemacount machine, leitz photometer, and EKF machine.

Insurance

For the insurance industry, appropriate buzz words highlight experience with contracts, claims, personal injury, workman's compensation, and assets. This includes knowledge of different areas of insurance, such as fire, theft, automotive, property, business, health, and disability. Familiarity with premiums, appraisals, policies, financial planning services, and insurance sales should also be included.

▶ **Buzz Words**
Accounts receivable
Auto insurance claims
Broad-based customer group
Caseload
Claims management services
Commercial and individual financial services
Credit associations
Credit insurance
Credit life insurance
Dental care services
Dental insurance firm

Disability income insurance
Emergency coverage
Estate planning
Financial and insurance operations
Health care delivery
Health plan coverage
High exposure claims
Investment planning
Lending organizations
Loss prevention
Malpractice insurance
Permanent insurance
Personal insurance
Product portfolio
Professional liability insurance
Professional medical services
Property and casualty reinsurance
Regional and specialty property and casualty insurers
Risk management programs
Search and examination services
Title insurance

▶ **Phrases to Use When Describing Your Skills and Experience**

- Evaluated client portfolios for claims; filed regarding personal injury and negligence.
- Worked as an actuary; computed premiums and insurance risks in conjunction with supporting team.
- Interacted with customers daily to explain annuity plans, real estate transactions, and claims.
- Adjusted premium rates for commercial and individual financial services; notified clients of renewal periods.
- Updated records regarding policies and procedures to be ready for use by real estate brokers.

- Recorded proof of loss and delivered reimbursement checks.
- Assisted individuals in selection of insurance policies. Worked to ensure lowest rates and highest coverage possible to fit individual needs.
- Computed settlements for homeowners after major disasters.
- Implemented employee wellness programs for special accounts during renewal periods.
- Conducted automotive claims investigations to determine net loss.
- Worked in professional liability insurance, advocating the rights of policy holders.

Legal and Protective Services

In these fields, buzz words highlight experience with interpreting and enforcing the laws. This includes supporting the legal system; patrolling and inspecting property to protect against theft, vandalism, and illegal entry; and ensuring the safety and security of persons who have been arrested, are awaiting trial, or who have been convicted of crimes and sentenced to serve time in correctional institutions. It also includes maintaining order, enforcing rules and regulations, and supplementing counseling.

▶ **Buzz Words**
Administrative support services
Attorney-client conferences
Clerical support
Community outreach
Copyright registration and licensing
Courtroom activity
Criminal investigations
Crisis intervention

Custody/traffic direction processes
Drafting wills
Extensive corporate dealings
Fire fighting
Fire prevention
Human services
Interviewing of witnesses
Legal research
Licensing
Medical documentation
Modernization of office procedures
Notarizing legal documents
Paralegal services
Permitting processes
Polygraph techniques
Preparation of cases
Prisoner visitation
Public utility litigation
Record filing
Resident and building security
Safety and crime prevention
Security programs
Training workshops
Trial preparation
Vandalism and theft deterrence
Weaponry training

▶ Phrases to Use When Describing Your Skills and Experience

- Prosecuted criminal cases at district court in conjunction with Urban Violence Strike Force.
- Prepared and presented civil and criminal motions before district and superior courts.
- Presented public-safety workshops and lectures.

- Supervised criminal investigations and trained assistant district attorneys.

Retail

Retail industry buzz words demonstrate experience in the sale of clothing, goods, or appliances, either directly to consumers or to the retail stores, or the buying of such products for sale in stores. They also demonstrate knowledge of customer service, handling transactions, complaints, and returns, and the management of a retail environment.

 Buzz Words

Accessories
Apparel
Appliances
Beauty care products
Brand names
Catalog retailer
Children's products
Consumer advocate
Design professionals
Direct marketing
Factory-direct
Fashion
Food services
General merchandise
Gross margin
Independently owned
Leading retailer
Marketing research
Mass merchandisers
National direct sales company
Price marketing

Promotional advertising

Retailer

Soft-goods products

Specialty retailer

Trade

Value-priced

Wholesale

▶ **Phrases to Use When Describing Your Skills and Experience**

- Explained brands of televisions, videos, cellular phones, computers, and other electronics to customers.
- Filled orders, shipped products, and answered calls for women's intimate apparel catalog retailer.
- Operated cash register, ringing both cash and credit card transactions, with responsibility for knowledge of discounted prices, clearance items, ad items, and changes in universal product codes (UPCs).
- Managed specialty fashion store carrying private label product lines of nationally recognized brands.
- Sold wide assortment of primary apparel in mall-based retail outlet at value prices.
- Bought women's, men's, and children's apparel for independently owned retail store.
- Excelled in suggestive selling of sales promotions, as well as customer service duties, such as layaways, returns, and exchanges.
- Organized shipments of accessories, stocked shelves by categories in different departments, and took inventory of all items annually.
- Oversaw all aspects of managing one location in major bookstore chain, including verifying barcodes, organizing category sections by book title, scheduling employees, and handling all accounting.

Science

For scientific positions, each particular field will have many specialized technical terms aside from those listed here. Science industry buzz words, in general, display experience with research and development. This includes research to develop new medicines; increase crop yield; improve the environment; study farm crops, animals, and living organisms; and explore practical use and knowledge of chemicals, as well as the atmosphere's physical characteristics, motions, and processes.

▶ **Buzz Words**
Agriculture
Air pollution
Animals
Bacteria
Biological research
Cleanup procedures
Drainage
Ecosystem
Firefighting techniques
Fisheries
Forecasting weather
Forestry
Geological aspects
Horticulture
Instrumentation
Materials research
Microprocessors
Mineral content
Natural disasters
Oceanic research
Pest control
Plant acquisition

Quality control systems

Raw material

Satellites

Soil testing

USDA regulations

Veterinary medicine

Waste disposal

Weather conditions

Wildlife activities

▶ Phrases to Use When Describing Your Skills and Experience

- Ensured smooth running of the lab and orderly maintenance of telescopes; ordered equipment and supplies.
- Conducted more than 500 manual and computerized assays of steroids, carcinogenic analysis, vitamins, fibrinogens, and other chemicals in hospital laboratory.
- Developed laboratory microcomputer systems for instrument automation and custom and specialized instrumentation/test equipment.
- Designed and built a continuous viscometer detector for gel permeation chromatography to provide absolute molecular weight and branching data.
- Performed set funnel extractions, creating surrogate solutions and maintaining laboratory inventory of glassware and chemicals, waste disposal, and cleanup.
- Managed the operation of a livestock and production farm, its marketing and accounting tasks, selling beef, lamb, and produce to supermarkets, restaurants, and roadside vegetable stands.
- Researched sources for tree and plant acquisition.
- Made written, editorial, and research contributions to ten briefing papers and a comprehensive management plan for Puget Sound.

- Worked directly with doctors of veterinary medicine and racehorse trainers in the breeding and grooming of top-quality thoroughbreds.

Technical

Technical industry buzz words highlight experience with applying specialized knowledge of technology, systems, engineering, and science. Potential applications for technical skills and experience exist in virtually all industries, including transportation, building design and inspection, engine repair and maintenance, electrical systems design, and communications.

▶ **Buzz Words**
Aircraft maintenance
Analytical attributes
Architecture
Artistic illustration
Blueprints
Building codes
Codes and standards
Compliance procedures
Data testing standards
Design development
Drafting
Drafting technology
Electrical regulations
Equipment application
Final product design
General construction
Hand tools
Hardware
Hybrid microcircuit design and drawing

Illustration
Inspection
Inventory
Lock repair
Maintenance
Mechanical aptitude
Multimedia product
Operations
Plumbing regulations
Product development
Quality assurance
Real estate development layout
State rules and regulations
System design
Technical drawing
Technical illustration
Technical writing
Troubleshooting
Zoning laws

▶ **Phrases to Use When Describing Your Skills and Experience**

- Trained in maintenance, servicing, and troubleshooting on all areas of aircraft from wing tips to landing gear, nose to tail, interior and exterior, including removals and replacements of component parts, repairs, lubrications, refueling, and flight-line launching and recoveries.
- Worked within both the public and private sectors. Required knowledge of local government agency procedures (e.g., obtaining permits and variances and interfacing with the building, planning, and engineering departments).
- Created and interpreted testing programs to evaluate and modify product performance and reliability for manufacturer of commercial kitchen equipment.

- Developed standard designs for retaining walls and rein-forced-concrete bridge abutments, the design of which are still currently being used.
- Used verbal specifications to develop electronic illustrations for new and changed products.
- Researched the effect of worldwide television deregulation on broadcast, cable, and satellite television, as well as inter-national broadcasting and advertising.

Transportation and Travel

In the transportation and travel industries, buzz words highlight experience with conveying passengers or goods, providing or controlling means for transportation, and coordinating or advancing the travel of others. They also include knowledge of various transportation methods, either from the customer service side or the transporting side.

 Buzz Words

Airports
Bus service
Cargo services
Charter services
Communities
Commuter train lines
Construction services
Cruise line
Dinner/theater events
Domestic travel
Emergency road services
Executive travel
Express services
Flat rate
Freight service railroad operations

Global transportation
High-speed rail
Highways
International travel
Light rail transit
Limousine transportation services
Mass transportation
Moving
Off-road divisions
Passenger service
Public transportation firm
Railroad industry
Safety policies and procedures
Sightseeing activities
Specialized transportation services
Subways
Tow services
Transportation services
Travel
Vacations
Vehicles
Warehousing
Weddings
Worldwide supply chain solutions

▶ **Phrases to Use When Describing Your Skills and Experience**

- Planned vacations and business trips, both foreign and domestic, for discount service travel agency.
- Confirmed ticket purchases, scheduled connecting flights, and contacted transportation services for passengers.
- Sold passes for incoming and outgoing trains, handled switching track operations, and was responsible for general managing of station.

- Mapped out route systems for buses in coordination with peak periods.
- Operated commuter rail, adhering to all mass transit regulations.
- Enforced safety policies and procedures for specialized vehicles.
- Programmed self-propelled vehicles and self-unloading bulk carriers; performed maintenance when necessary.
- Coordinated sightseeing activities, made restaurant reservations, and arranged other local services for tourists.
- Drove public shuttle bus on express service route with designated drop-off locations.
- Filed reports on average weekly traffic and planned traffic routes with fluctuating rush hour schedules.

Appendix A

Thank-You
Letters

The first thing you should do after an interview, after sending the interviewer anything he requested, is send a thank-you letter. Job searchers sometimes feel that sending a thank-you letter will make them seem like they are trying to "kiss up" to the interviewer. You don't have any reason to think that, because interviewers rarely see it that way. Sending a thank-you letter is a nice gesture that will let the interviewer know you appreciate the time he spent meeting with you. It will set you apart from other job candidates who choose not to send one.

Here are four sample thank-you letters. The first three are written to the actual interviewer, and the final one is written to an administrative assistant who showed the candidate around the office. This letter is significantly shorter than the others, and it does not make a point of reiterating any of the writer's skills, since its recipient will not be making the hiring decision and never discussed those skills with the candidate.

SAMPLE THANK-YOU LETTER #1

Joseph R. Green
14 Willow Street
Hoboken, NJ 07030

June 5, 2009

Ms. Maria Sanchez
Production Manager
Artistic Media
515 Madison Avenue
New York, NY 10022

Dear Ms. Sanchez:

Thank you for meeting with me this afternoon regarding the assistant production manager position at Artistic Media. I appreciate the time you spent getting to know me and explaining the specifics of the job.

I feel strongly that my experience and skills will allow me to make significant contributions to the production team. Artistic Media seems to be a company that values creativity, which is definitely one of my strengths.

I am looking forward to hearing from you within the week, as we discussed. Thank you again for your time and for considering me for this position. You can reach me by phone at (212) 555-4444 or by e-mail at *jgreene@rcat.net*.

Yours truly,

Joe Green

SAMPLE THANK-YOU LETTER #2

Beverly Smith
1524 South Jefferson Street
Williams, AZ 86046

September 21, 2009

Mr. Connor Shmedley
Customer Service Manager
Smart Mart Stores, Inc.
250 Adams Avenue
Flagstaff, AZ 86001

Dear Mr. Shmedley:

I appreciate your meeting with me this morning regarding the assistant customer service manager job at Smart Mart Stores. I enjoyed having the opportunity to talk to you about the improvements you have planned for the customer service department.

As I mentioned to you during the interview, before I moved to Williams, I worked at Bullseye Stores, which, as you know, has a great reputation for providing customer service. I worked closely with the department manager in implementing many of the procedures that earned Bullseye that reputation. I hope to have the opportunity to work with you to implement such procedures at Smart Mart.

Once again, thank you for taking time out of your busy schedule today. If you have any further questions, you can reach me by phone at (520) 555-5151 or by e-mail at *bevsmith@netco.com*. I look forward to hearing your decision soon.

Sincerely,

Beverly Smith

SAMPLE THANK-YOU LETTER #3

Sandy Beane
37 Oak Drive
Portland, OR 97205

June 24, 2009

Dr. Pat Lee
26 Tulip Street
Portland, OR 97201

Dear Dr. Lee:

Thank you for taking time out of your busy schedule this afternoon to interview me for the office manager position. I would welcome the opportunity to work with you and the members of your staff.

As you expressed in your interview, you are looking for someone who can manage a very busy office while showing compassion for your patients. As we discussed during the interview, though I did not work in a medical office, my experience managing a law office has provided me with the skills necessary to do this job well.

Again, thank you for meeting with me. If you have additional questions, you can reach me by phone at (503) 555-1234 or by e-mail at *sbeane@horizon.net*. I look forward to hearing from you regarding your decision.

Yours truly,

Sandy Beane

SAMPLE THANK-YOU LETTER #4

Rose Thornton
105 Peyton Place
Chicago, IL 60637

April 19, 2009

Mr. Richard Rheinhardt
Executive Assistant
Turning Corporation
1543 48th Street
Chicago, IL 60637

Dear Mr. Rheinhardt:

I just wanted to send a quick note to thank you for showing me around your offices on Tuesday after my interview with Janet Parker.

As Ms. Parker mentioned to you, I am interviewing for the bookkeeper position. Perhaps we will get to work together.

Yours truly,

Rose Thornton

Career-Related Websites

6FigureJobs

www.6figurejobs.com

Executives can post their resumes and search for jobs for free on this website.

About Career Planning

http://careerplanning.about.com

The Everything® Practice Interview Book author Dawn Rosenberg McKay's site covers all aspects of career planning including career choice, job hunting, job training, legal issues, and the workplace.

About Job Searching

http://jobsearch.about.com

Alison Doyle, the guide to this excellent site, helps you with all aspects of online job searching, writing resumes and cover letters, references, interviewing skills, and unemployment.

About Job Searching: Technical

http://jobsearchtech.about.com

Guide J. Steven Niznik keeps you updated on the technical job market. Get the latest information on health care, engineering, semiconducter, science, Internet, and telecom jobs.

CareerMag.com

www.careermag.com
At this site, you can search for jobs by career, industry, keyword, or location.

CareerBuilder.com

www.careerbuilder.com
Through its partnerships with newspaper publishers Tribune, Gannett, and Knight Ridder, CareerBuilder.com lists local jobs from newspaper help wanted sections from around the country. Search this huge jobs database by location, company, job type, and industry. You can even search in Spanish.

Career Journal

www.careerjournal.com
Career Journal is the *Wall Street Journal's* executive career site and is geared toward executives, managers, and professionals. It includes salary and hiring information, job search advice, and career management help. There is also a searchable database of jobs in select fields.

CollegeGrad.com

www.collegegrad.com
This job board targets college graduates and recent graduates. In addition to job listings, you'll find information on career choice, job search advice, and salary information.

Company Research from About Career Planning

http://careerplanning.about.com/cs/companyresearch
Find out what resources you can use to do company research. Learn how to access business directories and news sources.

The Equal Employment Opportunity Commission

www.eeoc.gov

Use this website to learn more about the laws that protect workers from discrimination at work.

ExecutivePlanet.com

www.executiveplanet.com

This website includes business culture guides for international businesspeople.

FlipDog.com

www.flipdog.com

FlipDog.com collects job announcements from company websites. Search for jobs by employer, keyword, and category. Post your resume.

JobStar Profession-Specific Salary Surveys

www.jobstar.org/tools/salary/sal-prof.cfm

Get salary information for dozens of professions.

Knock 'em Dead

www.knockemdead.com

Author Martin Yate's website includes information on constructing resumes and cover letters as well as webinars on all aspects of job searches.

Monster

www.monster.com

Search for jobs by location or job category. You can also enter key words to search by job titles, company names, and requirements. Post your resume online so employers can find you.

Monster Career Advice

http://content.monster.com

Resume and job interviewing tips, salary information, relocating advice, and diversity advice from Monster.com.

NewsLink

http://newslink.org

This site provides links to business journals around the country.

Occupational Outlook Handbook

www.bls.gov/oco/home.htm

Use this resource, published by the U.S. Bureau of Labor Statistics, to find out what workers do on the job. Learn about working conditions, training and education needed, employment outlook, salary, and expected job prospects for a wide number of occupations.

Public Service Employees Network

www.pse-net.com

You'll find links to local government job listings on this site.

Quintessential Careers

www.quintcareers.com

Get job search and career advice. You'll find links to job banks, career advice for teens and college grads, and tutorials to help you with job interviews and writing a resume and cover letter.

Riley Guide

www.rileyguide.com

Librarian Margaret F. Dikel has organized myriad sites that can help you with your job search.

Salary.com

www.salary.com

Get salary information for a variety of occupations.

SEC Filings and Forms (EDGAR)

www.sec.gov/edgar.shtml

The Securities and Exchange Commission requires publicly held companies to file information about finances quarterly and information about material events or corporate changes as they occur. You can retrieve this information from the EDGAR database.

USAJOBS

www.usajobs.opm.gov

This is the official website of the U.S. Federal Government. Job listings for all federal jobs are posted here. Post and store a resume that you can use to apply for jobs on this site.

Vault

www.vault.com

When you're preparing for a job interview, Vault.com is the place to go. You'll find company and industry profiles. There are message boards where employees share information about their employers. There's also a free job board that lists thousands of openings.

Yahoo! HotJobs

www.hotjobs.com

Search for a job by keyword, job category, or location. Post your resume and let employers find you. You can cut and paste your current resume or use Resume Builder to get help creating a new one.

Books

▶ Job Search

The Back Door Guide to Short-Term Job Adventures by Michael Landes. CA: Ten Speed Press, 2002.

Cyberspace Job Search Kit: The Complete Guide to Online Job Seeking and Career Information by Mary B. Nemnich and Fred E. Jandt. IN: JIST Works, 2001.

Federal Civil Service Jobs by Dawn Rosenberg McKay and Michele Lipson. NJ: Peterson's, 2002.

JobBank Series. MA: Adams Media, Annual.

Job-Hunting for the So-Called Handicapped or People Who Have Disabilities by Richard Nelson Bolles and Dale S. Brown. IN: JIST Works, 2001.

Knock 'em Dead 2010: The Ultimate Job Search Guide by Martin Yate. MA: Adams Media, 2009.

► **Cover Letters and Resumes**

101 Best Cover Letters by Jay A. Block and Michael Betrus. NY: McGraw-Hill, 1999.

101 Grade A Resumes for Teachers by Rebecca Anthony and Gerald Roe. NY: Barron's Educational Series, 2003.

201 Killer Cover Letters by Sandra Podesta and Andrea Paxton. NY: McGraw-Hill, 2003.

Ace the IT Resume! by Paula Moreira and Robyn Thorpe. CA: Osborne/McGraw-Hill, 2002.

Adams Cover Letter Almanac, MA: Adams Media, 1995.

Adams Resume Almanac, MA: Adams Media, 1994.

America's Top Resumes for America's Top Jobs by Michael Farr. IN: JIST Works, 2002.

Best Resumes for $100,000+ Jobs by Wendy S. Enelow. VA: Impact Publications, 1997.

Best Resumes for College Students and New Grads by Louise M. Kursmark. IN: JIST Works, 2003.

Blue Collar Resumes by Steven Provenzano. NJ: Career Press, 1999.

Knock 'em Dead Cover Letters, 8th ed. by Martin Yate. MA: Adams Media, 2008.

The Damn Good Resume Guide: A Crash Course in Resume Writing by Yana Parker. CA: Ten Speed Press, 2002.

Designing the Perfect Resume by Pat Criscito. NY: Barron's Educational Series, 2000.

The Edge Resume and Job Search Strategy by Bill Corbin and Shelbi Wright. IN: JIST Works, 2000.

The Everything® Cover Letter Book by Steven Graber. MA: Adams Media, 2000.

The Everything® Resume Book, Second Edition by Burton Jay Nadler. MA: Adams Media, 2003.

Expert Resumes for Computer and Web Jobs by Wendy S. Enelow and Louise M. Kursmark. IN: JIST Works, 2002.

Expert Resumes for Health Care Careers by Wendy S. Enelow and Louise M Kursmark. IN: JIST Works, 2004.

Expert Resumes for People Returning to Work by Wendy S. Enelow and Louise M. Kursmark. IN: JIST Works, 2003.

Gallery of Best Resumes by David F. Noble. IN: JIST Works, 2001.

Gallery of Best Resumes for People Without a Four-Year Degree by David F. Noble. IN: JIST Works, 2000.

The Insider's Guide to Writing the Perfect Resume by Karl Weber and Rob Kaplan. NJ: Peterson's, 2001.

Knock 'em Dead Resumes, 8th ed. by Martin Yate. MA: Adams Media, 2008.

Knock 'em Dead Cover Letters, 8th ed. by Martin Yate. MA: Adams Media, 2008.

Real Resumes for Financial Jobs edited by Anne McKinney. NC: Prep Publishing, 2001.

The Resume Catalog: 200 Damn Good Examples by Yana Parker. CA: Ten Speed Press, 1996.

Resume Magic by Susan Britton Whitcomb. IN: JIST Works, 2003.

Resumes That Get Jobs, 10th ed. edited by Ray Potter. NJ: Arco, 2002.

Resumes that Knock 'em Dead by Martin Yate. MA: Adams Media, 2002.

Sales and Marketing Resumes for $100,000 Careers by Louise Kursmark. IN: JIST Works, 2000.

Top Secret Executive Resumes: What It Takes to Create the Perfect Resume for the Best Top-Level Positions by Steven Provenzano. NJ: Career Press, 2000.

Vault Guide to Resumes, Cover Letters and Interviewing 2002 Edition by the editors of Vault. NY: Vault, 2001.

▶ Interview Etiquette and Style

Adams Job Interview Almanac, MA: Adams Media, 1996.

Business Etiquette: 101 Ways to Conduct Business with Charm and Savvy by Ann Marie Sabath. NJ: Career Press, 2002.

Chic Simple Dress Smart for Men: Wardrobes That Win in the Workplace by Kim Johnson Gross and Jeff Stone. NY: Warner Books, 2002.

Chic Simple Dress Smart for Women: Wardrobes That Win in the Workplace by Kim Johnson Gross and Jeff Stone. NY: Warner Books, 2002.

Emily Post's the Etiquette Advantage in Business by Emily Post and Peter Post. NY: HarperCollins, 1999.

Esquire's Things a Man Should Know About Handshakes, White Lies, and Which Fork Goes Where by Ted Allen and Scott Omelianuk. NY: Hearst Communications, 2001.

Gestures: The Do's and Taboos of Body Language Around the World by Roger E. Axtell and Mike Fornwald. NY: John Wiley & Sons, 1997.

Your Executive Image: How to Look Your Best and Project Success for Men and Women by Victoria A. Seitz. MA: Adams Media, 2000.

▶ **International Job Searching**

Best Resumes and CVs for International Jobs: Your Passport to the Global Job Market by Ronald L. Krannich and Wendy S. Enelow. VA: Impact Publications, 2002.

Dun and Bradstreet's Guide to Doing Business Around the World by Terri Morrison, Wayne A. Conaway, and Joseph J. Douress. NJ: Prentice Hall Press, 2000.

Global Etiquette Guide to Europe: Everything You Need to Know for Business and Travel Success by Dean Allen Foster. NY: John Wiley & Sons, 2000.

International Jobs: Where They Are and How to Get Them by Nina Segal and Eric Kocher. NY: Perseus Publishing, 2003.

▶ **General**

The 7 Habits of Highly Effective People by Stephen R. Covey. NY: Free Press, 1989.

Building Your Career Portfolio by Carol A. Poore. NJ: Career Press, 2001.

Communicate with Confidence by Dianna Booher. NY: McGraw-Hill, 1994.

The Everything® Get-A-Job Book by Steven Graber. MA: Adams Media, 2000.

Get Paid What You're Worth: The Expert Negotiators' Guide to Salary and Compensation by Robin L. Pinkley and Gregory B. Northcraft. NY: St. Martin's Press, 2003.

How to Say It at Work: Putting Yourself across with Power Words, Phrases, Body Language, and Communication Secrets, by Jack Griffin. NJ: Prentice Hall Press, 1998.

Kick off Your Career: Write a Winning Resume, Ace Your Interview, Negotiate a Great Salary by Kate Wendleton. NJ: Career Press, 2002.

Make a Name for Yourself: 8 Steps Every Woman Needs to Create a Personal Brand Strategy for Success by Robin Fisher Roffer. NY: Broadway Books, 2000.

Negotiating Your Salary: How to Make $1000 a Minute by Jack Chapman. CA: Ten Speed Press, 2000.

The Networking Survival Guide: Get the Success You Want by Tapping into the People You Know by Diane Darling. NY: McGraw-Hill, 2003.

Power Interviews: Job-Winning Tactics from Fortune 500 Recruiters by Neil Yeager and Lee Hough. NY: John Wiley & Sons, 1998.

The Smart Woman's Guide to Resumes and Job Hunting by Julie Adair King and Betsy Sheldon. NJ: Career Press, 1995.

SuperNetworking by Michael Salmon. NJ: Career Press, 2003.

Targeting the Job You Want by Kate Wendleton. NJ: Career Press, 2000.

Women for Hire: The Ultimate Guide to Getting a Job by Tory Johnson, Robyn Freedman Spizman, and Lindsey Pollak. NY: Berkley Publishing Group, 2002.

Glossary

Acceptance letter: A letter informing an employer of one's decision to accept a job offer.

Accomplishment: Something at which you succeeded as a direct result of your efforts.

Achievement: See *accomplishment.*

Americans with Disabilities Act (ADA): A federal civil rights law that was designed to prevent discrimination and enable people with disabilities to participate fully in all aspects of society.

Annual report: The primary document most public companies use to disclose corporate information to shareholders.

Background check: Used by prospective employers to verify the information included on a job candidate's resume or application, including work history and educational background. May also include looking at criminal records and credit history.

Behavioral interview: An interview during which the interviewer asks the job candidate to demonstrate her competencies by giving real-life examples of when she has used those competencies. This may be either a standalone entity or part of a regular job interview.

Benefits: The part of your compensation package that is in addition to salary. May include health and life insurance, personal days, vacation, pension plans, tuition assistance, and severance packages.

Body language: The nonverbal gestures and mannerisms used to interpret one's true feelings.

Career exploration: This step of the career-planning process involves gathering information about an occupation to make a decision regarding career choice.

Certified Professional Resume Writer (CPRW): A resume writer who is certified by the Professional Association of Resume Writers.

Chronological resume: A resume on which work experience is listed in reverse chronological order (that is, the most recent job is at the top of the list).

Civil Rights Act of 1964, Title VII: This federal law prohibits employment discrimination based on an individual's race, religion, sex, or national origin.

Civil service: Employment in the federal government, or in a state or local government.

Combination resume: A resume that combines the information included on both a functional and a chronological resume. Skills are emphasized, but an employment history is included.

Committee interview: See *panel interview.*

Competencies: A combination of your knowledge, skills, and abilities.

Confidentiality agreement: Part of an employment contract that prohibits an employee from disclosing confidential or sensitive information. Also referred to as a *nondisclosure agreement.*

Corporate culture: The shared values, goals, and practices that give a corporation its unique personality.

Cover letter: A letter sent along with a resume. The cover letter's purpose is to introduce the job seeker to the person who will be reviewing the resume and to express the candidate's interest in the job.

Curriculum vitae (CV): A summary of one's work experience that is much more detailed than a resume; includes academic background, publications, and other professional achievements.

Equal Employment Opportunity Commission (EEOC): The federal agency that oversees the enforcement of antidiscrimination laws.

Exempt employee: Refers to employees who are exempt from the overtime and minimum wage provisions of the Fair Labor Standards Act. Exempt employees are generally those working in executive, administrative, professional, or outside sales positions.

Fair Labor Standards Act (FLSA): U.S. law that establishes minimum wage, overtime pay, record-keeping, and child labor standards. These standards affect nonexempt full-time and part-time employees in the private sector as well as in federal, state, and local governments.

Family and Medical Leave Act (FLMA): Enacted in 1993, this federal law allows for a leave from work for the birth or adoption of a child or one's own illness or that of a family member.

Form 8-K: The form a publicly held company files with the SEC to report the occurrence of any material events or corporate changes.

Form 10-Q: A quarterly report that a publicly held company files with the SEC.

Functional resume: A resume on which skills are categorized by job function. Abilities are emphasized rather than work history.

Glass ceiling: A term that refers to the invisible barrier that certain groups, e.g., women and minorities, cannot pass to reach higher career levels.

Goal, long-term: A career or personal objective that can take from three to five years to complete.

Goal, short-term: A career or personal objective that can be reached in one to three years.

Group interview: A job interview during which a group of candidates are interviewed at the same time.

Hard skills: The skills you learned in school or through some other formal training. See also *soft skills.*

Hiring manager: The person for whom a job candidate will work if hired. The hiring manager interviews and selects the candidate.

Human resources (HR) department: The department in a company that is responsible for selection, hiring, and training employees. Sometimes referred to as the *personnel department.*

Illegal questions: Technically, the questions that a prospective employer cannot, by law, ask a job candidate. Often refers to questions used to gather information that the employer cannot use to make a hiring decision because of antidiscrimination laws. See also *Equal Employment Opportunity Commission.*

Informational interview: A meeting during which someone planning his or her career learns about a field of work from someone who has firsthand knowledge.

Internship: Term of practical experience in one's field of study under supervision. Interns are sometimes paid.

Interpersonal skills: The skills one uses to get along with others.

Job announcement: See *job posting.*

Job banks: Websites that list job openings and allow users to search through them by location, job type, and often keywords such as job title and employer. See also *resume banks.*

Job club: A group of people who meet to offer support to one another during the job search process. Usually help is offered regarding resume writing, job interviewing, and networking.

Job description: Provides details about a job, such as duties, requirements, and hours.

Job objective: The section of the resume that tells a prospective employer what type of job the candidate is seeking.

Job offer: An offer made to a job candidate by the prospective employer. The job offer usually includes specifics about the job, such as salary, benefits, hours, and starting date.

Job posting: A notice announcing that a job is available. It usually gives some details about the position and its requirements.

Job reference: Someone who the potential employer may contact to ask about a job candidate. Generally this person will be able to recommend that the employer hire this person.

Job reference list: A neatly formatted list of job references that includes names and contact information.

Mentor: One who provides guidance for a less-experienced colleague.

Mock job interview: A practice job interview, possibly videotaped.

Network: The group of individuals to whom one can turn for help.

Noncompete agreement: Part of an employment contract or a separate agreement that states that one will not compete with his or her employer. An employee may be asked to sign a noncompete agreement upon being hired. Also referred to as a *noncompete clause.*

Nondisclosure agreement: See *confidentiality agreement.*

Nonexempt employee: Refers to employees who are covered by the Fair Labor Standards Act. Nonexempt employees must receive overtime pay and the current minimum wage.

Panel interview: A job interview during which a group of people ask questions of the job candidate. Also referred to as a *committee interview.*

Personality inventory: A tool used to find out what personality type one fits into. Personality inventories are used as self-assessment tools.

Portfolio: A collection of work. A portfolio generally contains pictures, photographs, or writing samples, but it may include any work samples a job candidate wants a prospective employer to see.

Pregnancy Discrimination Act: Amends Title VII of the Civil Rights Act of 1964 to protect a woman from being discriminated against based on her pregnancy or related condition.

Privately held company: A company owned by individuals or groups of individuals.

Publicly held company: A company with shareholders who have a financial stake in the company.

Qualifications: The knowledge, skills, and abilities a job candidate must have to be hired for a particular position.

Reasonable accommodation: Adjustments or modifications provided by an employer to enable people with disabilities to enjoy equal employment opportunities.

Reference: See *job reference.*

Rejection letter: A letter informing an employer of one's decision to reject a job offer.

Resume: A short summary of one's work history and educational background. A resume is usually one page in length. See also *chronological resume, combination resume,* and *functional resume.*

Resume banks: Websites that allow users to post resumes so employers may search through them to find eligible applicants.

Salary history: A document included as an addendum to the resume. Lists salaries for each job on the resume.

Salary negotiation: The process a job candidate goes through to obtain the best possible compensation package.

Screening interview: The initial interview with a prospective employer. Usually someone from the human resources department will try to verify items on the candidate's resume, such as dates of employment and schooling.

Securities and Exchange Commission (SEC): The U.S. government agency that protects investors and maintains the integrity of the securities market.

Selection interview: The interview during which the hiring manager will try to determine if the applicant is the best-qualified job candidate.

Sexual harassment: Unwelcome sexual advances, requests for sexual favors, or other verbal or physical conduct of a sexual nature. Rejection of this conduct may have a negative effect on one's employment, work performance, or create an intimidating, hostile, or offensive work environment. Sexual harassment violates the Civil Rights Act of 1964.

Soft skills: Skills that aren't specific to any occupation, but instead enhance one's performance regardless of what one's actual job is. See also *hard skills.*

Stress interview: A technique sometimes used by interviewers to weed out job candidates who can't handle adversity. The interviewer purposely makes the candidate uncomfortable or anxious.

Thank-you letter: A letter the job candidate sends, following a job interview, to each person who participated in the job interview.

Transferable skills: Skills one has gathered through jobs, hobbies, volunteer work, or other life experiences that can be used in future jobs or in a new career.

Work history: Past jobs as described on one's resume.

Vita: See *curriculum vitae.*

Index